MONOGRAPHS OF THE
SOCIETY FOR RESEARCH IN
CHILD DEVELOPMENT

SERIAL NO. 225, VOL. 56, NO. 3, 1991

NATIONAL SURVEY OF PROBLEMS AND COMPETENCIES AMONG FOUR- TO SIXTEEN-YEAR-OLDS: PARENTS' REPORTS FOR NORMATIVE AND CLINICAL SAMPLES

THOMAS M. ACHENBACH
CATHERINE T. HOWELL
HERBERT C. QUAY
C. KEITH CONNERS

WITH COMMENTARY BY
JOHN E. BATES

AND A REPLY BY THE AUTHORS

D0905232

MONOGRAPHS OF THE SOCIETY FOR RESEARCH IN CHILD
DEVELOPMENT, SERIAL NO. 225, VOL. 56, NO. 3, 1991

CONTENTS

ABSTRACT

ACHENBACH, THOMAS M.; HOWELL, CATHERINE T.; QUAY, HERBERT C.; and
   CONNERS, C. KEITH. National Survey of Problems and Competencies
   among Four- to Sixteen-Year-Olds: Parents' Reports for Normative and
   Clinical Samples. With Commentary by JOHN E. BATES; and a Reply by
   the Authors. *Monographs of the Society for Research in Child Development*,
   1991, **56**(3, Serial No. 225).

We compared parent-reported problems and competencies for national
samples of 2,600 4–16-year-olds assessed at intake into mental health services and 2,600 demographically matched nonreferred children assessed in
a home interview survey. Parents responded to the ACQ Behavior Checklist,
which includes 23 competence items, three competence scales, 216 problem
items, eight syndrome scales, Internalizing, Externalizing, and total competence and problem scores. Most items and scales discriminated significantly
($p < .01$) between referred and nonreferred samples. There were important
sex and age differences in problem patterns, but regional and ethnic differences were minimal. Somewhat more problems and fewer competencies
were reported for lower- than upper-socioeconomic-status children. Referral rates were similar in the most urban and rural areas, but they were
significantly higher in areas of intermediate urbanization.
   Correlations of problem scores with those obtained 10 years earlier in
a regional survey and with surveys in other countries showed considerable
consistency in the rank order of prevalence rates among specific problems.
Apparently owing to its more differentiated response scales, the ACQ was
susceptible to respondent characteristics that reduced its discriminative
power below that of the Child Behavior Checklist.
   Comparisons of procedures for discriminating between the normal and
the clinical range supported the value of a borderline category for children
who are neither clearly normal nor clearly deviant. Interview data from the
survey sample yielded significantly higher ACQ problem scores for children
who had fewer related adults in their homes, those who had more unrelated

adults in their homes, those whose biological parents were unmarried, separated, or divorced, those whose families received public assistance, and those whose household or family members had received mental health services. Children who scored higher on Externalizing than Internalizing problems tended to have unmarried, separated, or divorced parents and to come from families receiving public assistance. However, among children whose household or family members had received mental health services, there were greater proportions of both Externalizing and Internalizing patterns than among other children.

I. INTRODUCTION

Much of the research on children's behavioral/emotional problems and competencies has been based on subjects who are apt to be quite unrepresentative of children in general. This is not surprising in light of the inherent complexities of such research and the difficulties of obtaining truly representative samples, especially for studying clinically significant variables. Nevertheless, it is risky to draw conclusions about children in general from unrepresentative samples assessed with procedures whose parameters in larger populations are unknown.

In previous research, we developed instruments for obtaining standardized ratings of children's behavioral/emotional problems and competencies for use by a variety of informants (Achenbach, 1978; Achenbach & Edelbrock, 1983, 1986, 1987; Goyette, Conners, & Ulrich, 1978; Quay & Peterson, 1975, 1987). These instruments make it possible to link findings on children in a particular study with findings on children in other studies. The instruments are now widely employed in research and clinical practice and have been used to obtain normative data on random samples from the general population (Achenbach & Edelbrock, 1981, 1986, 1987; Goyette et al., 1978).

A few items dealing with behavioral/emotional problems have been included in national surveys of children in Britain (Fogelman, 1976; Pringle, Butler, & Davie, 1966) and the United States (National Center for Health Statistics, 1982; Oliver, 1974; Roberts & Baird, 1971; Zill & Peterson, 1982). We are aware of no previous national surveys, however, that were designed to obtain highly differentiated assessments of children's behavioral/emotional problems and competencies or to determine the association of such variables with actual referral for mental health services. Considering the size and diversity of the population of the United States, we believe that it is important to determine the distributions of clinically significant competencies, problems, and syndromes assessed via practical, replicable, and generalizable procedures and to identify variations related to regional, demographic, and familial differences.

1

PRACTICAL ASSESSMENT OF SYNDROME CONSTRUCTS

To assess competencies, problems, and syndromes in a national sample, we needed an economical standardized procedure to tap a wide range of characteristics, using readily obtainable data. Numerous rating scales and questionnaires have been developed for assessing children's behavior. However, most of these have focused on a relatively narrow range of characteristics or have not been designed to operationalize specific constructs. We sought to advance the knowledge base by assessing empirically derived syndrome constructs as well as a broad range of specific problems and competencies likely to be important in their own right. We use the term "syndrome" in the statistical sense of a group of items found to co-occur in samples of subjects. The term does not necessarily imply a "disease" model or any other particular conception of the cause or underlying nature of childhood disorders.

The assessment instrument—the ACQ Behavior Checklist—was developed by Achenbach, Conners, and Quay (1983) to test and operationalize syndromes hypothesized on the basis of previous multivariate studies. It was also designed to include items likely to be clinically important even if they were not associated with particular syndromes. Most of the previous multivariate studies began with a potpourri of items that were then analyzed to see which items tended to occur together. As described further in Chapter II, we reviewed all available multivariate studies to identify syndromes that had received enough support to be worth testing further. We then assembled and field-tested items selected to operationally define the hypothesized syndromes. Thereafter, we tested the presence of these syndromes via principal components/varimax analyses of ACQs scored for clinical samples. We then compared the syndromes derived from the ACQ with those derived from American and Dutch versions of the Child Behavior Checklist (CBCL) scored for other clinical samples (Achenbach, Conners, Quay, Verhulst, & Howell, 1989). For those syndromes that were similar in the different analyses, we derived syndrome constructs consisting of items that were common to the versions of each syndrome obtained from the ACQ, American CBCL, and Dutch CBCL.

After deriving the syndrome constructs from the three parent rating forms, we performed similar analyses of parallel sets of problem items scored on the Teacher's Report Form (TRF) and Youth Self-Report (YSR) for clinical samples (Achenbach, 1991a). From the syndromes that had counterparts for children of both sexes and different ages in ratings by different informants, we identified common sets of problem items that were used to define *cross-informant syndrome constructs*. As explained in Chapter II, the ACQ provides operational definitions of these syndrome constructs in terms of parents' ratings. The ACQ versions of these syndromes constituted one focus for assessing subjects in the present study.

To determine whether certain syndromes were mutually associated to form higher-order groupings, we performed second-order factor analyses of the syndromes scored for clinical samples (Achenbach, 1991a). (Our choice of factor analysis here, rather than components analysis, was based on evidence for the superiority of factor analysis with small numbers of variables, such as our eight syndrome scales; Snook & Gorsuch, 1989). The second-order analyses yielded two broad-band groupings reflecting a distinction between anxiety, depression, somatic complaints, and withdrawal, on the one hand, and aggressive and antisocial behavior, on the other. Designated as "Internalizing versus Externalizing," this distinction has been found in many other studies, where it has been given labels such as "Personality Disorder versus Conduct Disorder" (Peterson, 1961), "Inhibition versus Aggression" (Miller, 1967), and "Overcontrolled versus Undercontrolled" (Achenbach & Edelbrock, 1978). The sums of item scores on the Internalizing syndromes and on the Externalizing syndromes provided an additional focus for assessing children in terms of these broad-band groupings of problems.

Because different levels of assessment may be useful for different purposes, the present study was designed to assess children at the following levels, ranging from molecular to molar: (1) specific problem and competence items; (2) narrow-band syndrome and competence scales; (3) broad-band Internalizing and Externalizing groupings; and (4) total problem and competence scores. The levels are interrelated in a hierarchical fashion, such that each of the higher levels comprises elements of the lower levels. All four levels were scored from the ACQ Behavior Checklist and were analyzed separately for reliability, discriminative validity, and correlates to achieve the aims stated in the following section.

AIMS OF THE PRESENT STUDY

To advance our knowledge of the distribution and correlates of specific competencies, problems, and syndromes among American children, the present study was designed to achieve the following aims.

1. *To test an inexpensive standardized procedure for obtaining data on a well-differentiated set of competencies, behavioral/emotional problems, and syndromes for a nationally representative sample of 4–16-year-olds, as reported by their parents or parent surrogates.*—As detailed in Chapter II, the assessment instrument was designed to tap problems and syndromes identified as particularly important in previous empirical research. Parents were selected as the informants

because they typically know more about their children over longer periods and more situations than any other adult informant. Furthermore, parents' views of their child's functioning are usually crucial in determining what, if anything, will be done to help the child.

We recognize that parents' reports correlate only modestly with children's self-reports and reports by other informants, such as teachers, mental health workers, and observers. However, meta-analyses show similarly modest correlations among reports by all these informants (Achenbach, McConaughy, & Howell, 1987). It thus seems clear that situational variations in children's behaviors, as well as differences between informants' perspectives, limit the degree of agreement between informants. Rather than regarding any single source as a "gold standard," we therefore view parents as only one of several sources from whom important assessment data can be obtained. However, the use of standardized procedures to obtain data on a nationally representative sample enables us to generalize conclusions involving this particular type and source of data to the national population.

2. *To identify associations between parents' reports and such variables as the child's age, sex, socioeconomic status (SES), region of the country, urbanization, ethnicity, parents' marital status, family size and constellation, child-care arrangements, and family mental health contacts.*—By analyzing these variables in relation to one another, we could determine which ones were independently associated with parents' reports of their children's problems and competencies. The use of several SES indices (occupation, education, income, and various combinations of these) also enabled us to determine which ones were most closely associated with the problems and competencies reported for children by their parents.

3. *To determine which competencies, problems, and syndromes were significantly associated with clinical referral.*—Although the items and syndromes were selected for ostensible clinical relevance, the study was designed to test the degree to which they were actually associated with referral by comparing nonreferred children in a representative general population sample with demographically matched children who were referred for mental health services.

4. *To compare findings with those of previous studies that have used similar items.*—Achenbach and Edelbrock (1981), for example, used a research design and many items similar to those of the present study, albeit in a sample restricted to the greater Washington, DC, area. Studies in Australia, the Netherlands, Puerto Rico, and Thailand that used Achenbach and Edelbrock's items and survey procedures offer a basis for cross-cultural comparisons. To avoid repetition, we will defer details of these and other relevant studies until we present the comparisons in Chapter VIII.

5. *To provide a basis for longitudinal reassessments designed to test the predictive*

power of specific problems, competencies, syndromes, scale scores, and family variables for subsequent functioning.—Since the initial study reported here, it has been possible to carry out a 3-year follow-up in which data were obtained from parents, teachers, and those of the subjects who were at least 11 years old at follow-up. Funding has been approved for an additional 3-year follow-up. Results will be reported as the analyses are completed.

II. METHOD

THE ACQ BEHAVIOR CHECKLIST

Excluding disorders that emerge in infancy, such as infantile autism, we reviewed all published studies that employed multivariate methods to identify syndromes among children aged 4–16 who were not mentally retarded or physically ill or handicapped. Table 1 lists descriptive titles for the 12 syndromes that we identified as having received enough support in previous studies to be worth testing via the ACQ. (Reviews of the relevant previous studies have been published by Achenbach, 1985; Achenbach & Edelbrock, 1978; and Quay, 1986.)

To tap the 12 hypothesized syndromes, items were culled from the Achenbach (1981) Child Behavior Checklist (CBCL), the Conners (1978) Parent Questionnaire (PQ), and the Quay-Peterson (1982) Revised Behavior Problem Checklist (RBPC). Some items were split or revised to make them more specific. The ACQ includes counterparts of 115 CBCL items, 43 PQ items, and 60 RBPC items (some items have counterparts on multiple instruments). It also has five items from the Child Behavior Checklist for Ages 2–3 (Achenbach, Edelbrock, & Howell, 1987) and three items from the Teacher's Report Form (TRF; Achenbach & Edelbrock, 1986). Fifty-five new items were added to assess problems not included in the existing instruments. Competence items were adapted from the CBCL to tap involvement in activities, social relationships, and school functioning. The draft ACQ and the contents of the hypothesized syndromes were then critiqued by the following psychologists and psychiatrists, who are well known for their research on child psychopathology: Dennis Cantwell, Anthony Costello, Elise Lessing, Jan Loney, Lovick Miller, Judith Rapoport, Michael Rutter, and David Shaffer. The wording of items was modified on the basis of consultants' suggestions and the consensus of the ACQ authors.

The draft of the ACQ resulting from the foregoing process was tested in three field trials in which parents of children being seen for mental health services were asked to fill out the ACQ, the CBCL, the PQ, and the RBPC

TABLE 1

HYPOTHESIZED MULTIVARIATE SYNDROMES

Aggressive Behavior
Anxious/Depressed
Attentional Problems with Hyperactivity
Attentional Problems without Hyperactivity
Delinquent Behavior
Mean (found only for girls)
Obsessive-Compulsive-Perfectionistic
Schizoid
Sex Problems
Socially Inept
Somatic Complaints
Unresponsive-Uncommunicative-Withdrawn

in counterbalanced order. The parents also filled out a questionnaire comparing the four instruments. Parents were drawn from the caseloads of 100 mental health clinicians distributed throughout the United States plus the Institute of Psychiatry in London. For each of the field trials, approximately one-third of the 100 clinicians requested participation by a parent of a child in their current caseloads.

After each of the first two field trials, the ACQ was revised in response to the parents' comments. By the third field trial, no further suggestions for important changes were obtained. The final version of the ACQ (App. A) has 21 competence items and 215 problem items, an open-ended item for scoring problems not specified elsewhere on the ACQ, and open-ended items for describing the best things and the parent's greatest concerns about the child. A four-step response scale was chosen for the problem items on the basis of preferences expressed by some parents in the field trials. The instructions for the problem items are as follows (see App. A):

> Below is a list of items that describe children. As you read each item, please decide whether it has been true of your child at any time during the *past two months*. Then circle the number that best describes your child:
> 0 = Never or not at all true (as far as you know)
> 1 = Once in a while or just a little
> 2 = Quite often or quite a lot
> 3 = Very often or very much

The ACQ can be self-administered by people having at least sixth-grade reading skills, or it can be administered by an interviewer. The competence items are scored as shown in Appendix B. They are summed to obtain a total competence score than can range from 0 to 24 for children not attending school and from 0 to 30 for children who are attending school. A total problem score is computed by summing the 0–3 scores on the 215 problem items. In addition, if a respondent uses the open-ended item 216 to report any problems not included among the 215 in the problem list, the highest score (1, 2, or 3) for the additional problems is added to the sum of scores for the 215 listed problems. The total problem score can thus range from 0 to 648.

DERIVATION OF SYNDROMES SCORED FROM THE ACQ

Although the ACQ was designed to tap the 12 syndromes listed in Table 1, not all the syndromes were supported by the principal components analyses of the ACQ clinical samples (Achenbach et al., 1989). Of the 12 hypothesized syndromes, the two designated "Attentional Problems without Hyperactivity" and "Obsessive-Compulsive-Perfectionistic" failed to receive sufficient support to be considered separate syndromes in parents' ratings of any sex/age group. This does not necessarily mean that such syndromes cannot be identified from other sources of data. Instead, it means that the analyses detailed by Achenbach et al. (1989) could not separate them clearly enough to be treated as separate variables in this *Monograph*. Two other syndromes—"Mean" and "Sex Problems"—were found for only a few sex/age groups and will not be dealt with here (Achenbach, 1991b, provides findings on these syndromes from other data). Another syndrome— originally designated "Socially Inept" but now called "Social Problems"—was well supported only in ACQ ratings of boys, but subsequent analyses of additional data (Achenbach, 1991a) have supported it well enough for both sexes to be included in the present report.

Cross-informant syndrome constructs.—The ACQ was designed to assess syndromes that can be scored from parents' ratings. However, following the initial derivation of syndromes common to parents' ratings on the ACQ, American CBCL, and Dutch CBCL, we developed cross-informant syndrome constructs corresponding to eight of the syndromes supported by the ACQ analyses. Each of the eight constructs comprises problem items that were common to syndromes derived separately from new principal components analyses of parents' ratings on the CBCL, teachers' ratings on the TRF, and self-ratings on the Youth Self-Report (YSR).

To derive the constructs, we first performed principal components analyses with varimax rotations of ratings of children of each sex within different age ranges (ages 4–5, 6–11, and 12–18 for the CBCL; 5–11 and 12–18 for the TRF; and 11–18 for the YSR). For each instrument, we identified syndromes that were obtained in the analyses for a majority of the sex/age groups. For each syndrome obtained in a majority of the groups scored on a particular instrument, we constructed a *core syndrome* that consisted of the items that loaded on versions of the syndrome for a majority of the sex/age groups. Next, we compared the core syndromes obtained from the CBCL, TRF, and YSR. Items that were common to the core syndromes for at least two of the three instruments were used to form the cross-informant construct for that syndrome.

Informant-specific versions of the cross-informant syndromes.—Each cross-informant construct represents what is common to versions of a syndrome found in ratings by different informants. Yet each type of informant may also be able to report certain problems that are not apparent to other informants. In establishing operational definitions for each syndrome in terms of ratings by each type of informant, we therefore retained items that loaded highly on the versions of the syndrome derived from ratings by that type of informant. For example, the item *Disobedient at home* loaded highly on the CBCL versions of the Aggressive Behavior syndrome for all sex/age groups. This item did not load highly on the Aggressive Behavior syndrome obtained from the YSR, however, and the item is not included on the TRF. Because it was so strongly associated with the Aggressive Behavior syndrome in parents' ratings, it is included in the scale for scoring the Aggressive Behavior syndrome from the CBCL.

ACQ versions of the parent-scored syndromes.—The ACQ includes counterparts of 115 of the CBCL's 118 problem items. The three CBCL problem items omitted from the ACQ are *Allergy, Asthma,* and *Smears or plays with bowel movements,* none of which was included in any version of the eight cross-informant syndromes. Some CBCL items were divided into two items on the ACQ, as exemplified by the division of the CBCL item *Lying or cheating* into the ACQ items *Cheats* and *Lies.*

To score the ACQ in terms of the parent-rated versions of the cross-informant syndromes, we summed the scores of the ACQ counterparts of the CBCL items that compose a particular syndrome. For CBCL items that have two ACQ counterparts, the ACQ item receiving the higher of the two scores for a particular subject was counted toward the syndrome score for that subject. Thus, for example, if a boy received a score of 1 for the ACQ item *Cheats* and a score of 2 for the ACQ item *Lies,* he would receive a score of 2 toward the syndrome on which the CBCL item *Lying or cheating* is scored. Table 2 lists the ACQ items scored on the eight syndromes derived from the CBCL. There is a close correspondence between these syndromes and the eight that received the strongest support in principal components/ varimax analyses of the ACQ (Achenbach et al., 1989). However, the names of some syndromes have been modified somewhat from the names listed in Table 1 and those used by Achenbach et al. (1989).

TABLE 2

ACQ ITEMS SCORED FOR EIGHT SYNDROME CONSTRUCTS

A. INTERNALIZING

Withdrawn	Anxious/Depressed
102.[a] Looks unhappy	32. Lonely
127. Prefers to be alone	38. Cries without good reason
135. Refuses to talk	69. Fears impulses
141.[a] Sad or depressed	72. Needs to be perfect
145. Secretive	73. Feels unloved
160. Shy, timid	74. Feels too guilty
168. Stares into space	75. Feels worthless
180. Sulks	102.[a] Looks unhappy
196. Underactive	110. Nervous, tense
210. Withdrawn	141.[a] Sad or depressed
	147. Feels persecuted
Somatic Complaints	150. Self-conscious
	181. Suspicious
29. Aches, pains	193. Fearful, anxious
30. Dizziness	212. Worries
31. Headaches	
33. Nausea	
34. Stomachaches	
116. Overtired	
128. Eye problems	
133. Rashes, skin problems	
203. Vomits	

B. NEITHER INTERNALIZING NOR EXTERNALIZING

Social Problems	Attention Problems
5. Acts too young for age	5. Acts too young for age
27. Too dependent	20. Can't concentrate
54. Doesn't get along with peers	23.[a] Can't sit still, squirms
81. Gets teased	35. Confused
113. Not liked by peers	40. Daydreams
117. Overweight	92. Impulsive
126. Poorly coordinated	109. Twitches
214. Prefers younger kids	110. Nervous, tense
	114.[a] Overactive
Thought Problems	125. Poor school work
	126. Poorly coordinated
21. Can't get mind off thoughts	168. Stares into space
88. Hears things	
136. Repeats acts	
142. Says strange things	
149. Sees things	
168. Stares into space	
176. Strange behavior	

TABLE 2 (*Continued*)

C. EXTERNALIZING

Delinquent Behavior	Aggressive Behavior
26.[a] Cheats	11. Argues
55. Doesn't feel guilty	18. Brags
83. Hangs around kids who get in trouble	19. Bullies, mean to others
	43. Destroys others' things
101.[a] Lies	47. Demands attention
140. Runs away from home	48. Destroys own things
152. Sets fires	50. Disobedient at home
172. Steals at home	51. Disobedient at school
174. Steals outside home	61. Jealous
182. Swears, obscene language	96.[a] Irritable
185. Talks or thinks about sex too much	105. Loud
	120. Physically attacks people
194. Truancy	144. Screams
200.[a] Uses alcohol	158. Shows off or clowns
201.[a] Uses drugs	169. Starts fights
202. Vandalizes with others	177.[a] Stubborn
213. Prefers older kids	179. Sudden mood changes
	186. Talks too much
	187. Teases other kids
	188. Temper tantrums
	190. Threatens

[a] Items that were paired with another item by counting the higher of the two scores.

INTERNALIZING AND EXTERNALIZING

As mentioned earlier, second-order analyses of the CBCL, TRF, and YSR were used to identify broad-band groupings of the cross-informant syndromes (Achenbach, 1991a). For the CBCL, TRF, and YSR clinical samples of each sex within each age range, scores for the eight syndromes were subjected to second-order principal factor analyses, with squared multiple correlations in the principal diagonal as communality estimates. The two largest factors in each solution were rotated to the varimax criterion for simple structure. Averaged across all groups, the following syndromes had the highest loadings on the Internalizing and Externalizing second-order factors, respectively, with the mean loadings shown in parentheses: *Internalizing*, Withdrawn (.784), Somatic Complaints (.690), Anxious/Depressed (.650); *Externalizing*, Aggressive Behavior (.791), Delinquent Behavior (.778). Table 2 lists the syndromes in order, starting with those having the highest mean loadings on the Internalizing factor, followed by the three syndromes that did not have consistently high loadings on either second-order factor, and ending with the syndromes having the highest mean loadings on the Externalizing factor. (In App. G, items from the Internalizing grouping are superscripted "I," while items from the Externalizing grouping are superscripted "E.")

For purposes of our analyses, the Internalizing score consisted of the sum of scores for the items of the three Internalizing syndromes. Analogously, the Externalizing score consisted of the sum of scores for the items of the two Externalizing syndromes. No items were scored on both the Internalizing and the Externalizing syndromes, and no item was scored on more than one Externalizing syndrome. Items 102 and 141 were both scored on the Withdrawn and Anxious/Depressed syndromes, but they were counted only once in the Internalizing score.

PROCEDURES FOR OBTAINING THE NORMATIVE SAMPLE

To obtain a normative sample of 4–16-year-olds living in the 48 contiguous states, we contracted with Temple University's Institute for Survey Research (ISR) to select 100 subjects of each sex at each age who would be representative of the U.S. population with respect to the following characteristics: (a) white, black, and English-speaking Hispanic ethnicity; (b) socioeconomic status (SES); (c) urban-suburban-rural residence; and (d) Northeast, North Central, South, and West (Southwest and West Coast) geographic regions.

A multistage sampling design was used to draw subjects from a national sampling frame maintained by ISR. The first stage of sampling employed 100 primary sampling units (PSUs) selected on the basis of probabilities derived from 1985 projected population sizes. In the second stage of sampling, 650 secondary sampling units (SSUs) were selected within the 100 PSUs on the basis of equal probabilities. In the third stage, listing areas (LAs) were selected within each SSU. Enumerators were sent to households in the LAs to obtain the age and sex of the children in each household. In the final stage, a sample stratified by sex and age was drawn within each PSU to obtain one child of each sex at each age from 4 to 16, for a total of 2,600 children.

Children were excluded from the survey if they were mentally retarded or had a serious physical illness or handicap or if no English-speaking parent or parent surrogate was available for the interview. If more than one eligible child resided in a household, the interviewer used a random number table to select the child designated by the lowest number that had not yet been used in that PSU. At the end of the interview, the respondent was asked whether the child had been taken to a psychiatrist, psychologist, social worker, guidance clinic, or other mental health service within the preceding 12 months. Children who met this criterion for referral to mental health services were excluded from analyses of the nonreferred sample but were used in other analyses that are detailed later. For each child who met the criterion for referral, an additional child was chosen from among children of the same age and sex residing in the same LA. If the interview with that child's parent showed that the child had not been referred, then that child served as a substitute for the first child in the nonreferred sample. In the one case where the second child was also found to be referred, the parents were interviewed about a third child.

To avoid obtaining only the most conveniently available subjects, enumerators were initially given only half the housing units in each LA, which were not enough to obtain all the needed subjects. The remaining units were assigned as needed. Additional housing units were assigned only after 90% of previously assigned units either had yielded a final result or had been visited five times without a final result. To avoid biasing the sample against working parents, all screening interviews were conducted on weekends or after 4:30 P.M. on weekdays. Most interviews were done between February and August 1986, but some were done in subsequent months in order to replace subjects whose data were found to be faulty or who were found to have duplicated cells that had already been filled. Respondents were not paid for the interviews. The survey sampling results are summarized in Table 3.

As Table 3 shows, 21,625 households were screened. The overall completion rate was 92.1% for interviews sought with parents of identified eligible children. If we multiply the total of 478 households that were not successfully screened by the 32.1% of screened households found to have eligible children, this yields an additional 153 hypothetical eligible children who might have resided in these households. If we add these 153 hypothetically missed children to the 2,986 known eligibles for whom interviews were sought, we obtain a total of 3,139 known and hypothetical eligibles. Divided into the 2,751 eligibles for whom interviews were completed, this yields a hypothetical lower-bound estimate of 87.6% of possible eligibles for whom interviews were completed.

Because of difficulties in obtaining data on enough subjects in some cells and discrepancies between the ages initially indicated for some subjects and the ages obtained through later verifications, the number of subjects was not exactly 100 in all cells. The largest shortfalls were for both sexes at age 16, where $N = 96$ boys and 95 girls. One 17-year-old of each sex was available to be added to the cell for 16-year-olds. From the pool of extra interviews obtained for previously filled cells, the best available substitutes for the missing 16-year-olds were three 15-year-old boys and four 14-year-old girls. At the other end of the age spectrum, one boy who was found to be 3 years old was retained in the 4-year cell with 99 boys who had reached

TABLE 3

Actual and Hypothetical Completion Rates of Interviews
in the National Survey

1. Target households screened	21,625
a) Households having eligible children, including those not interviewed because quota was filled	6,933
b) Percentage of households having eligible children	6,933/21,625 = 32.1
2. Results for households having eligible children:	
a) Interviews completed for quota of nonreferred children	2,600
b) Interviews completed for clinically referred children ...	88
c) Interviews for children in already filled strata	46
d) Faulty interviews deleted	+ 17
Total interviews for eligibles	2,751
e) Respondent refused interview for eligible child	+ 235
Total interviews sought for eligible children	2,986
f) Completion rate for interviews sought with eligible children	2,751/2,986 = 92.1
3. Target households not screened:	
a) No informant reached in five callbacks	80
b) Screening refused	190
c) Residents away for duration of survey	12
d) Other—locked building, seasonal housing	+ 196
Total households not screened	478
4. Calculation of hypothetical lower bound for completion rate:	
a) Total households not screened	478
b) Percentage of screened households having eligibles	× .321
c) Hypothetical missed eligibles	153
d) Actual eligible households	+ 2,986
e) Actual + hypothetical eligible households	3,139
f) Hypothetical lower bound for completion	2,751/3,139 = 87.6

their fourth birthday. Other than the cells for 16-year-olds and the compensating additions made to cells for 14- and 15-year-olds, only two cells deviated by as many as two subjects from the target N of 100 per cell.

INTERVIEW USED FOR THE NORMATIVE SAMPLE

Either parent of the target subject could serve as the respondent. In the absence of any biological, adoptive, foster, or stepparent, the interview was conducted with the legal guardian, if there was one. Otherwise, the person most responsible for the child served as the respondent. A letter describing the interview (App. C) was presented to the respondent, followed by a copy of the ACQ. The interviewer then asked each ACQ question and wrote down the respondent's replies. After completing the ACQ, the interviewer asked questions about the family composition, marital status of the child's parents or parent surrogates, child-care arrangements, family income, and mental health services received by family members (App. D).

Interviews were anonymous. To make follow-ups possible, however, the respondent was asked at the completion of the interview to provide identifying information and the names of two people who would know the family's location in the event of a move. ISR sent appreciation-verification letters to all respondents with a postpaid return form for verifying key details of the interview. If an interviewer's work was not adequately verified by responses to the letters, follow-up contacts were made to verify the interviews. Replacement interviews were conducted with other families if necessary. The data were keypunched and key verified by ISR staff and then checked in multiple ways by the study staff at the University of Vermont. Because discrepancies were found between some subjects' ages and their birth dates as given by respondents, these respondents were contacted for clarification. If the corrected age differed from that of the cell that the subject was intended to fill, an interview was obtained for a replacement subject if a replacement of the target age could be obtained from the identified eligibles at that site. Otherwise, the subject was placed in the cell appropriate for his or her age, resulting in some deviations from the target N of 100 per cell, as explained earlier.

PROCEDURES FOR OBTAINING THE CLINICAL SAMPLE

Because there are no adequate population data on American children receiving mental health services, it was not possible to establish a national sampling frame from which to draw a representative sample of referred children. Instead, we contracted with 18 clinical services distributed across the United States to have parents anonymously fill out ACQs at intake, according to the instructions shown in Appendix E. Children were to be excluded if they were mentally retarded (IQ < 75), had serious physical illnesses or handicaps, or were brought to the mental health service for reasons other than their own behavioral/emotional problems (e.g., for custody evaluations).

The 18 participating services (listed in App. F) included university and hospital clinics, free-standing guidance clinics, and private practices. Most children were candidates for outpatient services, but a few may have eventually become inpatients.

Although there is no way to ensure that our clinical samples are representative of all American children referred for mental health services, our 18 participating agencies encompassed clienteles that differed widely with respect to SES, ethnicity, geographic area, and urban-suburban-rural resi-

TABLE 4

<small>CHARACTERISTICS OF MATCHED NORMATIVE AND
CLINICAL SAMPLES</small>

Variable	Normative[a]	Clinical[a]
Hollingshead (1975) nine-point occupation scale for higher-status parent (1 = low, 9 = high SES):		
M	5.3	5.4
SD	2.2	2.0
Ethnic distribution (%):		
Non-Hispanic white	74.3	75.3
Black	15.8	16.4
Hispanic	6.5	1.3
Mixed, other	3.4	7.0
Region of country (%):		
Northeast	22.8	22.7
North Central	26.2	35.3
South	33.0	27.2
West	17.9	14.8
Interview respondent (%):		
Mother	80.2	87.7
Father	17.0	8.7
Other	2.8	3.6

[a] $N = 2,600$.

dence. All the major regions of the 48 contiguous states were represented. Several services were in large cities serving many minority and lower-SES clients (e.g., Downstate Medical Center in New York City; Washington, DC, Children's Hospital; Washburn Clinic, Minneapolis; Wilder Foundation, St. Paul). Others served small cities and rural areas (e.g., Maine Medical Center; University of Vermont; University of Iowa Pediatric Department Behavior Disorders Clinic; Mid-Missouri Mental Health Center). Others served small cities and suburban areas adjoining large metropolises (e.g., Morristown, NJ, Memorial Hospital; Worcester Youth Guidance Center). Still others were tertiary referral centers that saw cases referred from long distances (e.g., University of Minnesota Child Psychiatry; Stanford University Child Psychiatry). The nature of funding varied greatly within and between services, including unfunded cases, Medicaid, a variety of private insurance arrangements, and payment directly by families.

Data collection lasted from January 1983 until December 1987. ACQs lacking scores for more than eight problem items or important demographic data were excluded. If both parents were available, they were each asked to fill out a separate ACQ, but only one ACQ was used in the comparisons with the survey sample. From the ACQs completed for 5,364 clinical subjects, 2,600 were drawn for matching to the survey sample of 2,600 nonreferred children on the basis of age, sex, ethnicity, region of the country, and respondent (mother, father, other). Referred and nonreferred subjects were also matched as closely as possible according to lower-, middle-, and upper-SES levels, based on the Hollingshead (1975) occupational score for the parent having the higher-status occupation. This was the SES index found to be most strongly associated with problem scores, as detailed later in the section on SES indices.

Because of low referral rates at both ends of the age range, the closest demographic matches included one referred boy and two referred girls who had not yet reached their fourth birthday plus one referred boy and four referred girls who had reached their seventeenth birthday. The availability of only 60 referred 16-year-old and 93 referred 15-year-old girls who could be demographically matched to nonreferred girls also necessitated the use of an additional 43 14-year-old referred girls. Only one other cell deviated by as much as four subjects from the target N of 100 per cell. For simplicity, we will refer to an age range of 4–16, despite the inclusion of four 3-year-olds and seven 17-year-olds in the matched samples of 5,200 referred and nonreferred children. Table 4 summarizes the characteristics of the matched normative and clinical samples.

III. BASIC FINDINGS ON THE ACQ

TEST-RETEST RELIABILITY

To obtain an estimate of test-retest reliability, survey interviewers administered the ACQ twice to parents of 97 subjects in the normative sample at intervals ranging from 4 to 14 days ($M = 8.2$ days). The Time 1 − Time 2 r for total competence score was .91 and for total problem score was .88 (both $p < .001$), indicating good reliability in the rank order of scores. As shown in Table 5, the mean test-retest r of all scales was .82. The one-way intraclass correlation (ICC) for the mean Time 1 score versus the mean Time 2 score on individual competence items was 1.00 and for individual problem items was .97. This indicates high reliability according to a measure that reflects stability in the magnitude of mean scores on each item relative to the other items as well as in the rank order of scores for each item relative to the others.

There was no significant difference between any Time 1 versus Time 2 competence score, but there were significant declines in most problem scores, as shown in Table 5. The total problem score declined from a mean of 74.0 to 58.0 ($t = 7.72$, $p < .001$). Problem scores have been found to decline over brief intervals on many other rating and interview measures (Achenbach & Edelbrock, 1983; Edelbrock, Costello, Dulcan, Kalas, & Conover, 1985; Robins, 1985). The implications of a decline of this size will be addressed in Chapter V.

INTERPARENT AGREEMENT

ACQs completed separately by mothers and fathers of 94 children in the clinical sample yielded an interparent r of .72 ($p < .001$) for both the total competence score and the total problem score. (The 94 cases came from several clinical settings that asked both parents to independently complete the ACQ when both were available.) As Table 5 shows, the mean

TABLE 5

TEST-RETEST RELIABILITY AND INTERPARENT AGREEMENT FOR SCALE SCORES

SCALE	RELIABILITY[a] (N = 97)			AGREEMENT (N = 94)		
	r	M Time 1	M Time 2	r	M Father	M Mother
Competence:						
Activities	.80	6.9	6.9	.49	6.6	7.4**
		(2.4)	(2.3)		(2.1)	(2.0)
Social	.81	6.7	6.6	.75	4.7	4.4*
		(2.0)	(1.8)		(2.0)	(2.1)
School[b]	.87	5.0	5.0	.87	3.4	3.2*
		(1.0)	(1.0)		(1.5)	(1.4)
Total Competence[b]	.91	19.3	18.9	.72	15.0	15.0
		(3.9)	(3.8)		(4.0)	(3.9)
Problems:						
Withdrawn	.83	3.4	2.6**	.63	6.9	7.7
		(3.2)	(2.6)		(4.9)	(5.0)
Somatic	.84	1.5	1.0**	.67	3.0	4.1**
		(2.2)	(1.8)		(3.5)	(4.4)
Anxious/Depressed	.80	4.6	3.6**	.64	9.5	11.6**
		(4.0)	(3.9)		(6.9)	(7.8)
Social	.80	2.4	2.0*	.77	5.7	6.5*
		(2.3)	(2.3)		(4.2)	(4.8)
Thought	.76	1.1	.9	.45	2.5	3.2*
		(1.4)	(1.6)		(2.5)	(2.9)
Attention	.85	4.5	3.7**	.79	11.7	13.0**
		(3.9)	(4.2)		(6.7)	(7.4)
Delinquent	.73	2.1	1.7**	.84	6.1	6.4
		(1.8)	(2.0)		(5.2)	(5.2)
Aggressive	.79	11.4	8.8**	.78	21.3	23.0
		(6.4)	(6.2)		(12.4)	(13.5)
Internalizing	.87	9.2	6.9**	.62	18.3	22.1**
		(7.1)	(6.6)		(12.6)	(13.7)
Externalizing	.81	13.5	10.5**	.81	27.4	29.4
		(7.7)	(7.6)		(16.1)	(17.5)
Total Problems	.88	74.0	58.0**	.72	146.0	163.4**
		(41.9)	(41.5)		(76.5)	(80.9)
Mean r	.82			.72		

NOTE.—Reliability subjects were from normative sample. Agreement subjects were from clinical sample. All r's were significant at $p < .0001$. Numbers in parentheses are standard deviations.

[a] Mean interval = 8.2 days.

[b] Because subjects not attending school were not scored for School and Total Competence scales, $N = 65$ for reliability and 85 for agreement analyses of these scales.

* $p < .05$ for differences between means by paired t test.

** $p < .01$ for differences between means by paired t test.

interparent r for all scales was also .72, which is higher than the mean r of .59 between mothers' and fathers' ratings of children's problems found in meta-analyses of 31 previously published studies (Achenbach, McConaughy, & Howell, 1987). There was no difference between mean total competence scores reported by mothers and those reported by fathers, but mothers scored their children significantly higher than fathers on the Activities scale, six problem scales, and the total problem score ($M = 163.4$ vs. 146.0, respectively, $t = 2.88$, $p < .01$). Fathers scored their children significantly higher than mothers on the Social and School scales. The one-way ICC for the mean of mothers' versus the mean of fathers' scores on individual items was .99 for both the competence and the problem items.

As another way of comparing reports by mothers and fathers of clinically referred children, we identified cases where only the mother or only the father was available to complete the ACQ. Cases where mothers completed the ACQ were then precisely matched for age and sex to cases where fathers completed the ACQ. The cases were also matched as closely as possible for SES, ethnicity, and region of the country. We were able to find ACQs for 136 pairs of boys and 108 pairs of girls matched in this way, for a total of 488 ACQs, with half the ACQs completed by mothers and half completed by fathers.

We performed 2 (mothers vs. fathers) $\times$ 2 (girls vs. boys) $\times$ 6 (ages 4–5, 6–7, 8–9, 10–11, 12–13, 14–15, 16) $\times$ 4 (Northeast, North Central, South, West) ANCOVAs, with the covariates being white versus other, black versus other, and SES (Hollingshead, 1975, scores for parental occupation) on all scales. Only one out of the 15 analyses showed a significant difference between scores obtained from mothers and fathers. The one difference reflected higher scores by mothers than fathers ($p = .03$) on the Somatic Complaints scale. However, this is less than would be expected by chance in 15 comparisons (Sakoda, Cohen, & Beall, 1954). There were no significant interactions between sex of parent and any other variable. These findings indicated that overall scores reported by the parent who was the available informant in our clinical sample were not significantly affected by whether the parent was the mother or the father.

To determine whether mothers and fathers of nonreferred children differed in their reports, we identified ACQs completed by mothers and those completed by fathers of children in the normative sample who were precisely matched for age and sex and matched as closely as possible for SES, ethnicity, and region of the country. We were able to find ACQs for 214 pairs of boys and 212 pairs of girls matched in this way, for a total of 852 ACQs, with half the ACQs completed by mothers and half completed by fathers.

ANCOVAs like those comparing mothers and fathers of referred children on all scale scores showed no significant differences or interactions attributable to sex of parent. The great similarity between reports by mothers and those by fathers of nonreferred children indicated that the scale scores in our normative sample should not be affected by which parent was the informant.

CONCURRENT VALIDITY

We tested concurrent validity by computing r's between the final version of the ACQ and the three other instruments completed for 29 referred children having complete data from the final field trial. Note that, even though the ACQ contains counterparts of problem items from the three other instruments, it is by no means simply the sum of these instruments. The response scales, instructions, formats, wording of counterpart items, and item pools differ among the instruments. The ACQ total problem score showed an r of .88 with the Achenbach (1981) CBCL, .78 with the Quay-Peterson (1982) RBPC, and .68 with the Conners (1978) PQ (all $p < .001$). This indicates good concurrent validity with respect to total problem scores on widely used instruments differing in specific content and format.

COMPARISON OF SES INDICES

Although lower-SES groups are often reported to manifest more psychopathology and other problems than upper-SES groups (e.g., Achenbach, Verhulst, Baron, & Akkerhuis, 1987; Hollingshead & Redlich, 1958), there is no definitive SES index. To determine which of several possible SES indices was most closely associated with problems reported for children by their parents, we computed Pearson r's between total ACQ scores obtained by our normative sample and the following SES indices:

1. Occupation of the higher-status parent on Hollingshead's (1975) nine-step scale (to increase precision for occupations that could not be clearly categorized, we computed the mean of the two most likely categories);
2. Education of the better-educated parent on Hollingshead's seven-point scale, but modified to take account of rising educational levels by combining Hollingshead's two lowest levels into a single category of 9 or fewer years of schooling and adding a level to differentiate between postbaccalaureate degrees requiring less than 3 years (e.g., master's degrees) and those requiring 3 or more years (e.g., doctorates, law degrees);
3. The sum of unweighted scores 1 + 2;
4. The sum of weighted occupation and education scores for the

parent having the larger sum of the two weighted scores, using Hollingshead's weights of 5 for occupation and 3 for education;

5. The sum of 1 + 2 using Hollingshead's weights for the parent having the higher occupation score and the parent having the higher education score;

6. Hollingshead's five-level SES scale based on 4;

7. Hollingshead's five-level SES scale based on 5;

8. Total household income scored according to the nine categories shown in Appendix D; and

9. Per capita household income, computed by dividing the number used in 8 by the number of people living in the household.

After computing each of the SES scores 1–9 for the normative sample of 2,600 subjects, we computed r's between these scores and the total ACQ problem score separately for each sex at each year of age. To avoid effects on SES and problem scores that might be associated with minority group status, we also computed r's separately for non-Hispanic whites alone among boys aged 9, 14, and 16, these being the groups having the largest r's between SES and problem scores. In addition, because the total problem score could range far above the mean obtained by any group (216 problem items that could each be scored 0–3, range = 0–648), we wished to exclude the effects of outliers. We did this by computing the r's for only those subjects whose problem scores were within two standard deviations of their group's mean. Neither the exclusion of minority group subjects nor the exclusion of extremely high scorers had consistent effects on the size or direction of the r between total problem score and the SES indices. To choose among the SES indices, we therefore compared the r's that each SES index yielded with total problem score for the sample of each sex at each year of age as well as the mean of these r's across all sex/age groups.

Most of the nine SES measures correlated highly with each other. Six yielded the same overall mean r of $-.03$ between SES and total problem score, averaged across all 26 sex/age groups. The indices that yielded smaller mean r's were parental education and the two versions of Hollingshead's five-level SES scale. Based on the 2,600 subjects across whom the r's were averaged, there was thus a very small tendency ($p = .08$) for lower-SES parents to report more problems than upper-SES parents, according to most of the SES indices.

To provide finer-grained analyses of SES effects, we wished to use one of the SES indices as a covariate for analyses of individual ACQ items and total scores. As our index of SES, we selected the nine-point Hollingshead score for the higher-status parent's occupation because it was one of the six indices yielding the highest r with problem scores ($r = -.03$), it is less likely to be affected by regional and secular variations than are income and education, and it is more willingly and accurately reported by respondents than income or education. Furthermore, parental occupation was the SES index most commonly used in the previous studies that offer the best basis for comparison with our findings.

BEHAVIORAL/EMOTIONAL PROBLEMS IN REFERRED VERSUS NONREFERRED SAMPLES

To assess associations between ACQ problem scores and both clinical status and the major demographic variables, we performed analyses of covariance (ANCOVAs) on the scores for the 215 specific problem items, the open-ended item 216 for reporting additional problems, the eight syndrome scales, Internalizing, Externalizing, the difference between Internalizing and Externalizing scores (discussed later), and the sum of all 216 problem items. The samples consisted of the 2,600 referred and 2,600 nonreferred children described in Table 4.

ANCOVA design.—The ANCOVA design was 2 (referred vs. nonreferred) × 2 (boys vs. girls) × 7 (ages 4–5, 6–7, 8–9, 10–11, 12–13, 14–15, 16) × 4 (Northeast, North Central, South, West). The covariates were SES (Hollingshead occupation scores 1–9), non-Hispanic white versus other ethnic groups, and black versus other ethnic groups. Non-Hispanic white and black ethnic groups were chosen for contrast with all other ethnic groups because they were the largest. To provide an overview of the pattern of results for the problem scales, Figures 1–3 show the mean syndrome, Externalizing, Internalizing, and total problem scores for referred and nonreferred children of each sex at ages 4–16. As described later, Appendix G presents the detailed results of the ANCOVAs.

Correction for chance.—Because of the high statistical power afforded by the large sample size, we regarded effects as significant only if they reached $p < .01$. Furthermore, because there were 228 separate ANCOVAs (216 problem items, eight syndromes, Internalizing, Externalizing, Externalizing minus Internalizing, total problem score), we controlled for nominally significant effects that might arise by chance in such a large number of analyses. We did this by determining the number of $p < .01$ findings expected by chance in 228 comparisons, as specified by Sakoda et al. (1954). For example, seven out of the 228 F values for differences between clinically referred and nonreferred children could reach the .01 level of significance by chance (using a .01 protection level for the chance probability of reaching the .01 level). If no more than seven of the 228 comparisons of a particular type reached the .01 level, this could be considered a chance finding. However, for comparisons that showed more $p < .01$ differences than expected by chance, we have used superscript "g" in Appendix G to indicate those

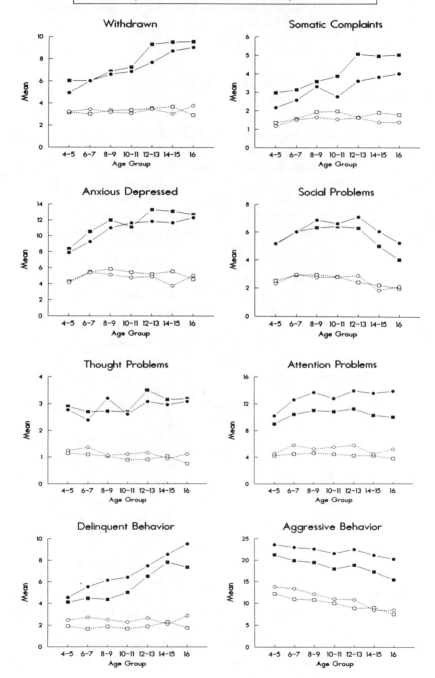

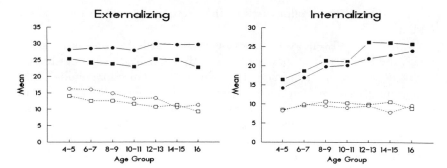

Fic. 2.—Mean Externalizing and Internalizing scores for referred and nonreferred children of each sex at each age.

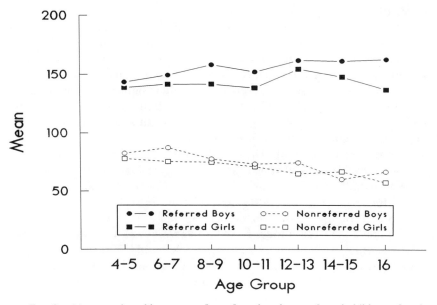

Fic. 3.—Mean total problem scores for referred and nonreferred children of each sex at each age.

Fic. 1.—Mean ACQ syndrome scores for referred and nonreferred children of each sex at each age.

that had the smallest F values because they were the most likely to be chance findings.

Effect sizes.—Even with our stringent standards for statistical significance, the high statistical power of our analyses enabled us to detect many effects of very small magnitude. To evaluate the relative magnitude of the significant effects, we therefore applied the following criteria suggested by Cohen (1988) for ANCOVA: effects accounting for 1%–5.9% of variance are small, 5.9%–13.8% medium, and greater than 13.8% large.

Clinical status.—As Appendix G shows, all the scale scores and 211 of the 216 items showed differences significant at $p < .01$ between referred and nonreferred children. The five items that did not reach our alpha criterion were (with p value for clinical status shown in parentheses): *2. Acts like opposite sex* ($p = .39$); *3. Acts silly or giggles too much* ($p = .04$); *94. Insists that certain things always be done in the same order* ($p = .06$); *154. Shows fear of strangers* ($p = .89$); and *192. Too concerned with neatness or cleanliness* ($p = .19$).

Two of the items—*10. Always on the go* and *24. Can't stand having things out of place*—showing $p < .01$ effects of clinical status were scored higher for nonreferred than referred children, although the difference accounted for less than .5% of the variance on both items. Because the F values for these items were among the seven smallest, their significant effects can be regarded as chance findings. Referred children obtained significantly higher scores on the remaining 209 items, all eight syndromes, Internalizing, Externalizing, and the total problem score.

As shown in Appendix G, clinical status had its largest effect on the Attention Problems syndrome and the total problem score, where it accounted for 22% of the variance, well above Cohen's (1988) minimum of 13.9% for large effects in ANCOVA. The mean total problem score was 72.7 (SD = 48.6) for nonreferred versus 149.3 (SD = 76.1) for referred children on a scale that ranges from 0 to 648. Clinical status also had large effects on the Withdrawn (16%), Anxious/Depressed (16%), Social Problems (14%), Delinquent (16%), and Aggressive (15%) syndromes as well as on the Internalizing (18%) and Externalizing (17%) scales. Medium effects of clinical status were found for the Somatic Complaints (8%) and Thought Problems (11%) syndromes.

The following eight items showed large effects of clinical status (greater than 13.8% of variance), with the percentage of variance indicated in parentheses: *20. Can't concentrate, can't pay attention for long* (18%); *50. Disobedient at home* (15%); *86. Has trouble following directions* (15%); *100. Lacks self-confidence* (17%); *125. Poor school work* (19%); *130. Punishment doesn't change his/her behavior* (17%); *141. Sad or depressed* (15%); and *195. Uncooperative* (14%).

Of the remaining items on which referred children obtained higher scores than nonreferred children, 70 showed medium effects of

5.9%–13.8% of the variance, 113 showed small effects of 1%–5.9%, and 18 showed effects accounting for less than 1% of the variance.

Sex differences.—As shown in Appendix G, significant sex differences were found on 130 of the 216 problem items as well as on five syndromes, Internalizing, Externalizing, and the total problem score. The only sex difference that exceeded Cohen's criteria for small effects occurred on item 7. *Admires tough guys,* where the tendency for boys to obtain higher scores accounted for 10% of the variance. Because the second largest sex difference accounted for only 4% of the variance in item *189. Thinks self too fat despite normal weight* (girls scored higher), it is possible that the 10% effect on item 7 was inflated by the word "guys," with its masculine connotation.

As shown by the superscript "M" in Appendix G, boys scored higher on 84 items, Attention Problems, Delinquent Behavior, Aggressive Behavior, Externalizing, and total problem score, including the one medium effect of sex differences, 24 small effects, and 64 effects accounting for less than 1% of the variance. Girls scored higher on the 46 items designated with superscript "F," Somatic Complaints, Anxious/Depressed, and Internalizing, including two small effects of sex differences and 47 effects accounting for less than 1% of the variance. Boys scored higher on significantly more items than girls ($p < .01$ by sign test). For the total problem score, boys obtained a mean of 115.7 (SD = 69.2), compared to a mean of 106.8 (SD = 73.3) for girls. Although this difference was highly significant at $p < .0001$, it accounted for only .4% of the variance.

Age differences.—Appendix G shows that there were significant age differences on 172 items, Withdrawn, Somatic Complaints, Anxious/Depressed, Social Problems, Attention Problems, Delinquent Behavior, Aggressive Behavior, Internalizing, and Externalizing but not on the total problem score. The largest age effect accounted for 13% of the variance in item *208. Whines,* where younger children obtained the highest scores. Other items that met Cohen's criteria for medium effects included *125. Poor school work* (7%, older children higher); *129. Pulls at the hands or clothes of adults* (9%, younger higher); *163. Smokes tobacco* (9%, older higher); *170. Stays out late at night* (9%, older higher); *194. Truant, skips school* (8%, older higher); and *200. Uses alcohol without parents' approval* (8%, older higher). Of the remaining age effects, 101 were small, and 72 accounted for less than 1% of the variance. Younger children obtained significantly higher scores on 80 items, Social Problems, Aggressive Behavior, and Externalizing (superscript "Y" in App. G), older children on 61 items, Withdrawn, Somatic Complaints, Anxious/Depressed, Delinquent Behavior, and Internalizing (superscript "O"), and there were significant nonlinear effects of age on 31 items and Attention Problems (superscript "NL").

Regional differences.—Our ANCOVAs showed differences among regions of the country on 72 items, Withdrawn, Anxious/Depressed, Attention

Problems, Delinquent Behavior, Aggressive Behavior, Internalizing, Externalizing, and the total problem score. The largest effect of region was found for *182. Swears or uses obscene language,* but this effect accounted for only 1% of the variance. It reflected a tendency for parents in the South to score their children slightly but significantly lower than parents in all other sections of the country and parents in the Northeast to score their children lower than parents in the North Central and Western regions (all differences $p <$ .01). The second largest regional effect was .8%, reflecting lower scores for the South than any other region on *169. Starts fights* (all $p <$ .01). No other regional effect accounted for more than .7% of the variance. On the total problem score, there was a .3% regional effect, with children in the West obtaining slightly but significantly higher scores than children in the Northeast and South (both $p <$ .01). The number of interactions of region with sex and age did not exceed the seven expected by chance, and no interactions between region and other variables accounted for more than .8% of the variance. Furthermore, in the survey sample, there was no significant difference between regions in the proportion of children who had received mental health services during the preceding 12 months, $\chi^2(3) = 6.54, p =$ .09. Because regional effects were thus negligible, we have omitted them from the display of effects on problem scores in Appendix G.

Interactions between clinical status, sex, age, and region.—As shown in Appendix G, there were significant clinical status × sex interactions on 64 items, Withdrawn, Somatic Complaints, Attention Problems, Aggressive Behavior, and Externalizing but not on Internalizing or the total problem score. The largest clinical × sex interaction accounted for only .9% of the variance in item *51. Disobedient at school,* which reflected a somewhat larger effect of clinical status for boys than girls. No other clinical × sex interactions accounted for more than .6% of the variance.

Significant interactions between clinical status and age were found on 98 items, on all syndromes except Aggressive Behavior, and on the Internalizing, Externalizing, and total problem scores, as shown in Appendix G. The largest clinical × age interaction accounted for 5.2% of the variance in item *194. Truant, skips school,* which fell below Cohen's criterion of 5.9% for medium effects. It reflected larger effects of clinical status for older than younger children. A similar interaction was found for items *163. Smokes tobacco* (4% of variance), *200. Uses alcohol without parents' approval* (3%), and *201. Uses drugs for non-medical purposes* (3%). The 2% interaction effects on the Withdrawn and Delinquent Behavior syndromes and 1% effect on Internalizing also reflected larger effects of clinical status for older than younger children. An additional 21 items and Internalizing showed small clinical × age interactions, while 73 items, five syndromes, Externalizing, and the total problem score showed interactions that accounted for less than 1% of the variance.

Significant interactions between sex and age were found for 13 items, with the largest accounting for 1.9% of the variance in item *189. Thinks self too fat despite normal weight* and 1.5% of the variance in item *7. Admires tough guys*. On item 189, the interaction involved proportionately higher scores for older girls than boys, while, on item 7, it involved proportionately higher scores for younger boys than girls. All the remaining sex × age interactions accounted for less than .7% of the variance.

Region showed significant two-way interactions with clinical status on 30 items and two syndromes, but all accounted for less than 1% of the variance. Region also showed significant three-way interactions with age and clinical status on 18 items, but none accounted for more than 1% of the variance. Because the remaining two-way, three-way, and four-way interactions did not exceed the numbers expected by chance, they are omitted from Appendix G, as are the interactions of sex with age and region with clinical status.

SES differences.—As shown in Appendix G, significant SES effects were found on 116 items and on all syndromes except Anxious/Depressed as well as on the Internalizing, Externalizing, and total problem scores. The significant SES effects reflected higher problem scores for lower-SES than upper-SES children, except on items 8, 9, 72, 75, and 119 and Internalizing. However, none of the SES differences accounted for more than 1% of the variance: the tendency for lower-SES children to obtain higher scores accounted for only .3% of variance in the total problem score.

Ethnic differences.—Significant ethnic effects were found on 40 items, Social Problems, Attention Problems, Aggressive Behavior, Externalizing, and total problem score for the covariate non-Hispanic white versus other groups. Non-Hispanic whites were scored higher than other groups on 34 of the items, the three syndromes, Externalizing, and total problem score. The significant but tiny effect on total problem score accounted for less than .1% of variance. The largest effect of ethnicity accounted for .8% of the variance in item *192. Too concerned with neatness or cleanliness,* where scores were lower for non-Hispanic whites than for other groups. No other effect of this covariate accounted for more than .4% of the variance. The covariate for black versus other ethnic groups had significant effects on 19 items, all accounting for less than 1% of the variance. Blacks were scored higher than other groups on six of the 19 items. Because of their small size, ethnic effects are omitted from Appendix G.

DIFFERENCES BETWEEN INTERNALIZING AND EXTERNALIZING SCORES

The relative predominance of Internalizing or Externalizing problems may have important implications for services as well as informative associations with other variables. We therefore sought to determine whether differences between Internalizing and Externalizing problems were associated with clinical status, sex, age, region, SES, or ethnicity. To create similar metrics for Internalizing and Externalizing problems, we transformed the Internalizing problem scores into z scores across the entire sample of 5,200 subjects and likewise for Externalizing scores. Thus, each subject had a z score for Internalizing problems and a z score for Externalizing problems. As a result of the z transformation, the mean of all subjects' scores was .0 for Internalizing and .0 for Externalizing, with a standard deviation of 1.0 for each type of score.

As an index of the degree to which Internalizing versus Externalizing problems were reported for each subject, we computed a difference score ("E-I score") by subtracting the subject's Internalizing z score from his or her Externalizing z score. Subjects who had higher Externalizing than Internalizing scores thus obtained positive E-I scores, whereas subjects who had higher Internalizing than Externalizing scores obtained negative E-I scores.

We performed a 2 (clinical status) × 2 (sex) × 7 (age) × 4 (region) ANCOVA on the E-I scores, with SES, non-Hispanic white versus other, and black versus other as covariates. As shown in Appendix G, there was no significant difference between the E-I scores for referred versus nonreferred children in general. However, significant ($p < .01$) main effects showed that boys and younger children obtained higher E-I scores (Externalizing scores greater than Internalizing scores) than did girls and older children. The effect of sex accounted for 3% of the variance, while the effect of age accounted for 4%. These findings are summarized in Figure 4.

The two-way interactions of clinical status with sex, age, and region for E-I scores were significant at $p < .01$, although they all accounted for less than 1% of the variance. The clinical status × sex interaction reflected the fact that the scores of referred boys were the most Externalizing (mean E-I score = .21) whereas the scores of the referred girls were the most Internalizing (mean E-I score = −.28). The nonreferred boys (mean E-I = .08) and nonreferred girls (mean E-I = −.10) were intermediate between the referred samples of each sex, although the nonreferred samples of each sex also differed significantly from each other ($p < .01$). Thus, the general tendency for boys and girls to differ in E-I scores was especially pronounced in the referred samples, where boys' scores at all ages were more Externalizing and girls' scores above age 7 were more Internalizing than in the nonreferred samples, as shown in Figure 4.

The clinical status × age interaction reflected the fact that a linear age trend found for both the referred and the nonreferred samples was more extreme in the referred sample. Computed across clinical status, the test for

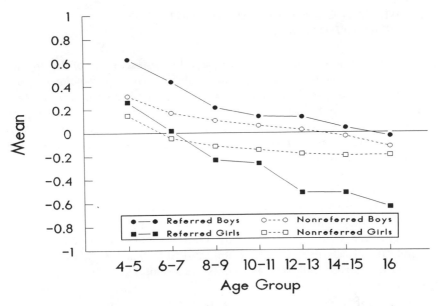

FIG. 4.—Mean Externalizing minus Internalizing z scores for referred and nonreferred children of each sex at each age.

the linear age trend was highly significant, $F = 147.89$, $p < .001$, owing to a progression from higher Externalizing scores at younger ages to higher Internalizing scores at older ages. However, in the nonreferred sample, the progression was from a mean E-I of .23 at ages 4–5, to .06 at ages 6–7, to .00 at ages 8–9, followed by a steady drop to $-.15$ at age 16. In the referred sample, the much steeper progression started from a mean E-I of .42 at ages 4–5, to .20 at ages 6–7, to $-.03$ at ages 8–9, and to $-.07$ at ages 10–11, followed by a drop to $-.29$ at age 16. Thus, just as with the contrast between boys and girls, age differences between Externalizing and Internalizing that were present in the nonreferred sample were much more pronounced in the referred sample, as can be seen in Figure 4.

The clinical status × region interaction reflected the tendency for referred children in the North Central region to have significantly more Externalizing scores than referred children from the Northeast or West, where Internalizing scores were greater than Externalizing scores.

Significant ($p < .01$) effects of the covariates SES and black versus other ethnicity indicated slightly higher E-I scores for lower-SES children and black children. However, both these effects accounted for only .1% of the variance. The three-way and four-way interactions were not significant.

BEHAVIORAL/EMOTIONAL PROBLEMS IN NONREFERRED
SAMPLE ANALYZED SEPARATELY

The selection of our survey sample to be representative of the 48 contiguous states enabled us to test demographic effects for the national population of nonreferred children. To determine whether such effects would differ from those found when the referred and nonreferred samples were analyzed together, we performed 2 (sex) × 7 (age) × 4 (region) ANCOVAs on all problem items, syndromes, Internalizing, Externalizing, E-I, and the total problem score for the 2,600 nonreferred children, with SES, non-Hispanic white versus other ethnic groups, and black versus other ethnic groups as covariates. These ANCOVAs thus paralleled the ANCOVAs summarized in Appendix G, except for the exclusion of clinically referred children and the resulting absence of the clinical status factor.

The ANCOVAs of nonreferred children revealed considerably fewer significant effects of sex, age, region, and SES than the ANCOVAs that included referred children, as follows: 92 versus 138 effects of sex, 137 versus 180 effects of age, 43 versus 77 effects of region, and 41 versus 127 effects of SES. Significant effects of ethnicity in the nonreferred sample were about the same as in the ANCOVAs that included referred children (45 vs. 45 effects of non-Hispanic white versus other and 13 versus 19 effects of black versus other). Significant effects occurred in one three-way interaction and in fewer interactions of region with sex and age than the seven expected by chance. There were 12 significant interactions between sex and age, compared to 13 in the ANCOVAs that included referred children. None of the interactions or ethnic effects exceeded 2% of the variance.

The lower statistical power afforded by 2,600 than 5,200 subjects is unlikely to account for much of the decline in the number of significant effects because the basic cell sizes were the same and the comparisons across cells were of asymptotically high power, as indicated by the similar numbers of significant interactions and ethnic effects with $N = 2,600$ and 5,200. The more numerous effects of sex, age, region, and SES found with $N = 5,200$ probably reflected the greater variance contributed by the high scores of the referred children.

Our findings indicated no significant effects of sex, interactions, SES, or black versus other ethnicity on total problem scores for the general population sample of nonreferred children. Younger children obtained significantly higher total problem scores than older children, an effect accounting for 2% of the variance. There was a regional effect in which children in the North Central region scored highest (less than 1% of variance). And non-Hispanic whites obtained higher scores than other ethnic groups (less than 1% of variance).

Of the significant sex effects on 86 items, five syndromes, and Externalizing, all but three were similar to those listed in Appendix G for the ANCOVAs including referred children. The three additional items showing significant sex effects in the nonreferred sample were *142. Says strange things or expresses strange ideas, 143. Says things that don't make sense* (both effects were less than 1% and reflect higher scores for boys), and *186. Talks too much* (the effect was less than 1% and reflects higher scores for girls). Just as in the ANCOVAs summarized in Appendix G, boys scored higher than girls in significantly more of the comparisons showing significant sex differences (73 vs. 19, $p < .01$ by sign test).

Of the 138 significant age effects, nine had not been significant in the ANCOVAs including referred children. Of these nine, the following accounted for 1% or more of the variance: *26. Cheats* (a 1% effect, younger children scored higher); *88. Hears things that aren't there* (1%, younger higher); *101. Lies* (2%, younger higher); Externalizing (3%, younger higher); and total problem score (3%, younger higher).

Of the 43 significant effects of region in the nonreferred sample, 11 were on scores that showed no significant regional effects in the ANCOVAs including referred children. However, the largest of these accounted for only .7% of the variance in item *107. Mumbles instead of speaking clearly*, which was highest in the West.

Only five of the 41 significant SES effects were on scores that did not show significant SES differences in the ANCOVAs that included referred children. All accounted for .5% or less of the variance and reflected higher scores for upper-SES children on items 18, 47, 87, and 212 and for lower-SES children on item 207. Except for the much smaller number of SES effects than when referred children were included (41 vs. 127), findings on the nonreferred sample were similar to those of the analyses including referred children, in that most SES effects indicated slightly higher scores for low-SES children.

In summary, ANCOVAs of the nonreferred general population sample showed the same minimal ethnic and interaction effects and fewer sex, age, regional, and SES effects than when the referred children were included. For nonreferred children in the 48 contiguous states, it can thus be concluded that problems reported by parents do not vary much by ethnicity, SES, or region. The parent-reported problems do vary more with the sex and age of the child, however.

COMPETENCE SCORES IN REFERRED VERSUS NONREFERRED SAMPLES

To assess differences in competence scores, we performed 2 (referred vs. nonreferred) × 2 (sex) × 7 (age) × 4 (region) ANCOVAs like those performed on the problem items. We performed similar ANCOVAs on the total competence score and the following three scales:

1. *Activities scale.*—Computed by summing *IA. Number of sports, IIA. Number of activities, IIIA. Number of jobs,* and the mean of responses to items *IB.* and *IC. Participation and skill in sports, IIB.* and *IIC. Participation and skill in activities,* and *IIIB. Job performance;*

2. *Social scale.*—Computed by summing *IVA. Number of organizations, IVB. Mean of participation in organizations, VA. Number of friends, VB. Contacts with friends,* the mean of *VIA. Behavior with siblings, VIB. Behavior with other children,* and *VIC. Behavior with parents* and the mean of *VID. Works alone* and *VIE. Plays alone;* and

3. *School scale.*—Computed by summing *VIIA. Mean academic performance, VIIB. (No) Special class, VIIC. (No) Grade repetition,* and *VIID. (No) Other school problems.*

Analyses of school items excluded children under the age of 6 and those not attending school.

As with the problem items, we determined the number of findings expected to be significant by chance in each set of competence scores. For each set of 27 comparisons (23 items, three scales, and total competence score), two comparisons would be expected to be significant at $p < .01$ by chance, using a .01 protection level (Sakoda et al., 1954). Where we found more significant differences than expected by chance, we have used superscript "i" in Table 6 to indicate those that had the smallest F values because they are the most likely to be chance findings.

The open-ended item VIII for describing the best things about the child and item IX for indicating what concerns the respondent most about the child were not included in any scale or the total competence score in these analyses. Figures 5 and 6 display the patterns of competence scale and total scores for referred and nonreferred children of each sex at ages 4–16, while Table 6 displays detailed findings from the ANCOVAs of competence scores. Note that the total competence score for ages 4–5 excludes the School scale.

Clinical status.—As indicated in Table 6, all but item *IIIA. Number of jobs* showed significant differences between referred and nonreferred children, as did the three competence scales and the total competence score. The differences favored the nonreferred children, except on item *IA. Number of sports* (.2% of the variance, likely to be a chance finding because it had one of the two smallest F values) and *IIA. Number of activities* (.7% of the variance). Five of the effects were large: *VIIA. Mean academic performance* (17%); *VIID. (No) Other academic problems* (23%); Social scale (16%); School scale (25%); and total competence (17%). Six other effects were medium, nine were small, and the rest accounted for less than 1% of the variance.

Sex differences.—Fifteen of the competence items, the School scale, and total competence showed significant sex differences. As Table 6 indicates, girls obtained higher scores on 12 items, the School scale, and total competence, while boys obtained higher scores on items *IA. Number of sports, IB. Participation in sports,* and *VB. Contacts with friends.* The only sex differences large enough to qualify as small effects were on *IA. Number of sports* (boys higher, 1% of variance), *VIID. (No) Other school problems* (girls higher, 2% of variance), and the School scale (girls higher, 2% of variance).

Age differences.—Age differences were larger and more numerous than sex differences, being significant on all scales and items except *IIC. Skill in activities,* as shown in Table 6. *IVA. Number of jobs* showed a medium effect of 7% that reflected higher scores for older children. Of the remaining significant effects, 10 were small, and 15 accounted for less than 1% of the variance. Younger children obtained higher scores on six items, the School scale, and the total competence score. Older children obtained higher scores on seven items and the Social scale. The age effects were nonlinear on nine items and the Activities scale.

Regional differences.—As Table 6 shows, we found significant regional effects on 13 of the competence items, the Activities scale, School scale, and total problem score. However, the largest regional effects accounted for only 2% of the variance in item *IIIA. Number of jobs* and the Activities scale, which is based partly on item IIIA. Children in the North Central region and the West obtained significantly higher scores on both these activities variables than children in the Northeast and South. On item *IIA. Number of activities,* children in the South scored significantly lower than children in the other three regions, while children in the West and North Central regions scored significantly higher than those in the Northeast, an effect accounting for 1% of the variance. The remaining regional effects accounted for less than 1% of the variance.

Interactions between clinical status, sex, age, and region.—Of the 162 analyses of interactions among clinical status and the three demographic variables, 27 showed significant effects. Only 17% of the analyses thus showed significant interactions, and all these effects accounted for less than 1% of the variance. Table 6 displays the significant effects for clinical status × sex (four effects); clinical status × age (10 effects); and clinical status × region (six effects). As there were only three significant effects for sex × age and sex × region and only two significant effects for age × region, these are omitted from Table 6. The interaction effects were all too small to have much substantive importance for the interpretation of competence scores.

SES differences.—Significant SES differences were found on 21 of the 23 competence items, the three competence scales, and the total competence score. The significant effects reflected more favorable scores for upper-SES children, with the exception that upper-SES parents more often entered

TABLE 6

PERCENTAGE OF VARIANCE ACCOUNTED FOR BY SIGNIFICANT ($p < .01$) EFFECTS OF CLINICAL STATUS, SEX, AGE, REGION, ETHNICITY, AND SES ON SOCIAL COMPETENCE SCORES

ITEMS[a]	CLINICAL STATUS[b]	SEX[c]	AGE[d]	REGION[e]	INTERACTIONS[f] C×S	C×A	C×R	COVARIATES SES[g]	Ethnicity[h]
IA. Number of sports (I)	< 1[C,i]	1[M]	5[NL]	< 1[NC]	…	< 1[i]	< 1	< 1	…
IB. Participation in sports	2	< 1[M]	< 1[NL]	…	…	< 1	…	< 1	…
IC. Skill in sports	1	< 1[F]	1[O]	< 1[W]	…	…	…	< 1	…
IIA. Number of activities (II)	< 1[C]	…	5[Y]	1[W]	…	…	…	2	…
IIB. Participation in activities	< 1[i]	…	1[Y]	< 1[W]	…	…	…	2	…
IIC. Skill in activities	< 1	…	…	< 1[W]	…	…	…	2	…
IIIA. Number of jobs (IV)	…	…	7[O]	2[W]	…	…	…	< 1	…
IIIB. Job performance	…	< 1[F]	1[O]	< 1[W]	…	…	…	…	…
IVA. Number of organizations (III)	< 1	…	6[O]	< 1[NC,i]	…	< 1	…	5	< 1[W]
IVB. Participation in organizations	2	…	4[O]	…	…	< 1	…	3	< 1[W]
VA. Number of friends (VI)	9	< 1[F,i]	< 1[O]	< 1[Si]	…	…	…	< 1[i]	< 1[W,i]
VB. Contacts with friends (V2)	4	< 1[M]	< 1[NL,i]	…	…	…	…	< 1[i]	< 1[W,i]
VIA. Behavior with siblings (VIA)	6	< 1[F]	< 1[Y]	…	< 1[i]	…	…	< 1	…
VIB. Behavior with peers (VIB)	11	< 1[F]	< 1[O]	…	< 1[i]	…	< 1	< 1	< 1[NW,i]
VIC. Behavior with parents (VIC)	12	< 1[F,i]	< 1[NL]	…	…	…	…	< 1	…

36

VID. Works alone (VID)	9	$<1^F$	$<1^{NL}$	$<1^W$	...	...	...	<1
VIE. Plays alone (VID)	5	...	$<1^Y$	$<1^Y$	...	...	...	$<1^i$
VIIA. Academic performance (age ≥ 6) (VIII)	17	$<1^F$	1^Y	1^S	...	<1	...	3
VIIB. (No) Special class (age ≥ 6) (VII2)	6	$<1^F$	$<1^{NL}$	...	...	<1	<1	<1
VIIC. (No) Repeat grade (age ≥ 6) (VII3)	2	$<1^F$	2^Y	$<1^{NE}$	...	...	...	3
VIID. (No) School problems (age ≥ 6) (VII4)	23	2^F	$<1^{NL}$	...	<1	...	$<1^i$	...
VIII. Best things about child	3	...	$<1^{NL}$	$<1^{NC}$	...	$<1^i$	$<1^i$	<1
IX. (No) Concerns about child	3	$<1^F$	$<1^{NL,i}$	...	...	...	$<1^L$	$<1^{NW}$
Activities scale	<1	...	$<3^{NL}$	2^W	...	...	...	3
Social scale	16	2^O	2^O	...	...	<1	<1	3
School scale (age ≥ 6)	25	2^F	$<1^Y$	$<1^S$	<1	<1	...	2
Total competence (age ≥ 6)	17	$<1^F$	$<1^Y$	$<1^S$	...	<1	...	5

NOTE.—Numbers in table indicate percentage of variance accounted for by each independent variable and covariate where the effect was significant at $p < .01$.

[a] For exact wording, see App. A. Numbers in parentheses refer to the numbers that counterpart items bear on the CBCL.

[b] Nonreferred children had higher scores on all items except IA and IIA.

[c] F = higher scores for females; M = higher scores for males.

[d] O = higher scores for older children; Y = higher scores for younger children; NL = nonlinear age effect.

[e] NC = highest scores for North Central region; W = highest scores for western region; S = highest scores for southern region.

[f] C × S = clinical status × sex; C × A = clinical status × age; C × R = clinical status × region. Other interactions were minimal and are discussed in text.

[g] All significant SES effects reflect higher scores for higher-SES children, except item IX.

[h] W = non-Hispanic white higher; NW = non-Hispanic white lower.

[i] Not significant when corrected for the number of analyses.

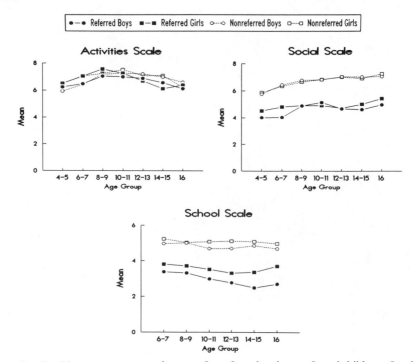

FIG. 5.—Mean competence scale scores for referred and nonreferred children of each sex at each age (School scale not scored for ages 4–5).

concerns on the open-ended item IX. The largest SES effects were 5% on item *IVA. Number of organizations* and on the total competence score. The other three scale scores and six items also showed effects defined by Cohen as small, while 14 items showed effects that accounted for less than 1% of the variance.

Ethnic differences.—The covariate scored for black versus all other ethnic groups showed only two significant effects. Because this is no more than expected by chance, we have not listed them in Table 6. However, as Table 6 shows, the covariate scored for non-Hispanic white versus all other ethnic groups yielded eight significant effects. These reflected more favorable scores for non-Hispanic whites in six comparisons and less favorable scores in two. None of the ethnic effects accounted for more than .5% of variance.

COMPETENCE SCORES IN NONREFERRED SAMPLE ANALYZED SEPARATELY

To assess the demographic effects on competencies in our representative nonreferred sample, we performed 2 (sex) × 7 (age) × 4 (region)

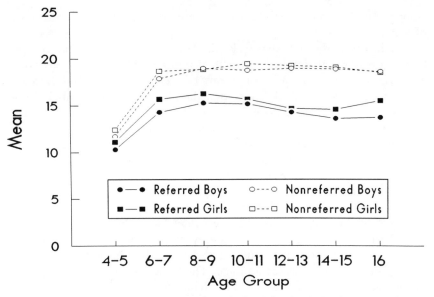

Fig. 6.—Mean total competence scores (excluding School scale for the 4–5 age group) for referred and nonreferred children of each sex at each age.

ANCOVAs on all competence items, the three competence scales, and the total competence score for the 2,600 nonreferred children. SES, non-Hispanic white versus other ethnicity, and black versus other ethnicity served as covariates. These ANCOVAs thus paralleled the ANCOVAs of the 5,200 children summarized in Table 6, except for the exclusion of clinically referred children and the resulting absence of the clinical status factor.

The significant effects of sex, age, region, and SES on competence items and scale scores were somewhat less numerous in the ANCOVAs of the 2,600 nonreferred children than in the ANCOVAs including the 2,600 referred children, as follows: *sex effects,* 11 significant effects in the ANCOVAs of 2,600 versus 17 significant effects in the ANCOVAs of 5,200; *age effects,* 14 versus 26; *region effects,* 12 versus 16; and *SES effects,* 22 versus 25. The magnitudes and directions of the effects found in the nonreferred sample were generally similar to those shown in Table 6 for the ANCOVAs that included referred children. However, the SES effects were larger in several of the ANCOVAs for nonreferred children, especially the following: *academic performance,* 7% in the ANCOVA of 2,600 versus 3% in the ANCOVA of 5,200; *School scale,* 6% versus 2%; and *total competence score,* 8% versus 5%. Unlike the problem scores, some of the competence scores thus appeared somewhat more strongly related to SES in the normative sample than when referred children were included. This suggests that, among troubled children, these scores are more uniformly low, regardless of SES.

Eight items, the Activities scale, the Social scale, and the total competence score showed significant effects of non-Hispanic white versus other ethnicity. This compares with significant effects on five items and the same scales in the ANCOVAs that included the clinical sample. Non-Hispanic whites were scored more favorably than other ethnic groups in 10 of the significant comparisons and less favorably in the other two. The effects on the Social scale and total competence score accounted for 1% of the variance, while the other significant effects accounted for less than 1% of the variance. There were significant effects of black versus other ethnicity on items *VA. Number of friends* (blacks higher) and *VB. Contacts with friends* (blacks lower), the Social scale (blacks lower), and the total competence score (blacks lower), but all accounted for less than 1% of the variance.

There were no significant three-way interactions or interactions between age and region, only one significant interaction between sex and region, and one between sex and age. These interactions were fewer than the two significant effects expected by chance for each type of analysis, and both accounted for less than 1% of the variance.

CLINICAL VERSUS SURVEY CONTEXT FOR DATA COLLECTION

The foregoing analyses show that parents of clinically referred children scored their children significantly higher on nearly every problem item and less favorably on nearly every competence item than parents of nonreferred children. We wished to know, however, whether the difference between the context of clinical intake versus home interview survey could have accounted for the differences between scores. To find out, we compared the 88 children identified in our survey as receiving mental health services in the previous 12 months with 88 survey children who had not received mental health services in the previous 12 months and 88 from our clinical sample. The three groups were precisely matched for age, sex, and non-Hispanic white versus other ethnic groups. The groups did not differ significantly in SES, $F < 1$, or proportion from each region, $\chi^2(6) < 1$, or whether the mother, father, or someone else completed the ACQ, $\chi^2(4) = 4.34, p = .36$.

To compare the three groups, we performed one-way ANCOVAs on their total ACQ problem and competence scores, with SES as a covariate. The ANCOVAs yielded significant F values of 40.21 and 42.16, both $p < .01$. LSD contrasts revealed that the mean problem score of the nonreferred subjects was significantly lower than that of the referred subjects identified in the survey (74.0 vs. 141.0, $F = 40.21, p < .01$). The mean competence score of the nonreferred subjects was also significantly higher than that of the referred subjects identified in the survey (19.2 vs. 18.1, $F = 11.25$, $p < .01$). The problem scores of the two referred groups did not differ significantly from each other, $F = 3.67$, $p > .05$, but the competence scores of the referred children identified in the survey were significantly higher than those in the clinical sample, $F = 32.65$, $p < .01$. These findings indicate that the less favorable scores for children in the clinical sample than for nonreferred children in the survey sample were not artifacts of the clinical versus home survey context in which the ACQs were completed. The intermediate scores of the referred children identified in the survey could reflect improvement since their referral for help, which spanned the previous 12 months, whereas the children in our clinical sample were assessed at intake, before they had received mental health services.

IV. SUMMARY OF FINDINGS FOR PROBLEM AND COMPETENCE SCORES

We believe that the present study provides data on a more extensive range of problems and competencies assessed in a more representative national sample over a wider age range than any previously published study. The survey sample was carefully selected to be representative of the population of the 48 contiguous states with respect to SES, ethnicity, geographic region, and urban-suburban-rural residence. It was stratified to yield one randomly selected boy and girl at each age from 4 to 16 living in 100 primary sampling units (PSUs) distributed throughout the United States. The actual completion rate of 92.1% for identified eligible subjects was very high, as was the theoretical lower-bound completion rate of 87.6% estimated by including hypothetical eligibles who might have been missed. Although there is no way to ensure representativeness of a national clinical sample, our clinical sample was obtained from diverse mental health services and was demographically very similar to our normative sample.

The 8-day test-retest r's of .88 for total problems and .91 for total competence on the ACQ indicate good reliability in the rank ordering of individual scores obtained on two occasions over periods when the target behavior was not actually apt to change much. The interparent r of .72 for total problems was higher than the mean r of .59 found between ratings of children's problems by parents in meta-analyses of 31 previously published studies (Achenbach, McConaughy, & Howell, 1987). Concurrent validity r's were .88 with the Achenbach (1981) CBCL, .78 with the Quay-Peterson (1982) RPBC, and .68 with the Conners (1978) PQ. This indicates good concurrent validity with a variety of widely used instruments differing in specific content, formats, and response scales.

The good psychometric properties of the ACQ, as well as the quality of our normative and clinical samples, provide a unique opportunity for advancing our knowledge of children's behavioral/emotional problems and competencies, as reported by their parents. We will initially summarize findings with respect to the particular problems, syndromes, and competencies assessed in the current study and relevant previous studies. We will then consider the use of problem and competence scores to discriminate between children who are most likely to be in the normal and those likely to be in the clinical range. Thereafter, we will consider findings with respect to family variables, comparisons with other studies, and the implications for research and services.

SUMMARY OF ACQ FINDINGS ON BEHAVIORAL/ EMOTIONAL PROBLEMS

As shown in Appendix G, referred children obtained significantly ($p < .01$) higher scores on 209 of the 216 problem items, all eight syndrome scales, Internalizing, Externalizing, and the sum of all ACQ problem items. Of the seven items on which referred children did not score significantly higher, five showed differences that did not reach $p < .01$, whereas two were scored significantly higher for nonreferred than referred children. One of the two items scored higher for nonreferred children, *10. Always on the go,* was included in the DSM-III criteria for Attention Deficit Disorder with Hyperactivity (American Psychiatric Association, 1980, p. 44) but has been omitted from DSM-III-R (American Psychiatric Association, 1987). Because item 10 and the other item scored higher for nonreferred children—*24. Can't stand having things out of place*—were among the seven yielding the smallest F values, their $p < .01$ effects for clinical status can be regarded as being within chance expectations. Nevertheless, our findings indicate that these items should definitely not be considered signs of pathology in parents' reports on their 4–16-year-old children.

Among the 209 items on which referred children scored significantly higher, eight showed effects of clinical status that were large by Cohen's (1988) criteria, that is, greater than 13.8% of the variance. These items were *20. Can't concentrate, can't pay attention for long, 50. Disobedient at home, 86. Has trouble following directions, 100. Lacks self-confidence, 125. Poor school work, 130. Punishment doesn't change his/her behavior, 141. Sad or depressed,* and *195. Uncooperative.* Clinical status also showed large effects on the Withdrawn, Anxious/Depressed, Social Problems, Attention Problems, Delinquent, and Aggressive syndromes, Internalizing, Externalizing, and total problem score, accounting for 14%–22% of the variance. Seventy items and the other two syndromes showed medium effects of clinical status, ranging from 5.9% to 13.8% of the variance.

The 22% effect of clinical status on the Attention Problems syndrome was as large as the effect on the total problem score and considerably larger than the next largest effect of clinical status on syndromes, which was 16% on both the Anxious/Depressed and the Delinquent syndromes. The very large effect of clinical status indicates that the Attention Problems syndrome is more strongly associated with referral than any of our other empirically identified syndromes, across all ages, both sexes, and different regions of the country. Two items of this syndrome also showed larger effects of clinical status than any other items. These were items *20. Can't concentrate, can't pay attention for long* (18% of variance) and *125. Poor school work* (19%). The strong empirical association between parent-reported attention problems and referral for mental health services is thus commensurate with the proportionately large clinical literature on these problems.

There was a significant, though small, tendency for lower-SES children to score higher than upper-SES children on many problem items. Ethnicity and region of the country showed fewer effects than SES on the problem scores, and these effects were very small. The minimal effects of SES, ethnicity, and region were borne out in the ANCOVAs of the nonreferred sample. On the whole, then, parents' responses to the ACQ problem items discriminated very well between demographically matched referred and nonreferred children. For the effect size associated with each problem score, the reader is referred to Appendix G.

Our finding that survey children who had been referred for mental health services within the previous 12 months obtained significantly higher problem scores and lower competence scores than matched nonreferred survey children demonstrates that the results were not artifacts of the clinical versus survey context. Similar findings from comparisons between Dutch CBCL scores for a clinical sample versus referred and nonreferred survey samples also argue against contextual artifacts (F. C. Verhulst, personal communication, June 17, 1988).

Sex, age, and clinical status patterns in problem scale scores.—Figure 1 depicts mean syndrome scores for children grouped by sex, age, and clinical status. As is evident from the figure, all three Internalizing syndromes (Withdrawn, Somatic Complaints, Anxious/Depressed) showed a pattern in which scores were similar for nonreferred children of both sexes at all ages, but scores for referred children increased with age, with referred girls scoring higher than referred boys.

The Social Problems and Thought Problems syndromes showed less consistent relations to sex, age, and clinical status. The Attention Problems syndrome and both Externalizing syndromes, by contrast, showed higher scores for boys than girls at nearly all ages for both the referred and the nonreferred samples. The age patterns differed among these three syndromes, however, with no linear age trend for Attention Problems, a significant increase with age for Delinquent Behavior, and a significant decrease with age for Aggressive Behavior. Thus, moving across the spectrum from the Internalizing to the Externalizing syndromes, referred girls tended to have higher Internalizing scores than referred boys, there were no consistent sex differences for Social Problems and Thought Problems, and boys scored higher than girls on the Attention Problems, Delinquent, and Aggressive syndromes. These patterns were also manifest in the Internalizing and Externalizing scale scores shown in Figure 2. The sex and age differences in total problem scores were minimal, however, as shown in Figure 3.

The contrasting Internalizing and Externalizing patterns in relation to sex, age, and clinical status are especially highlighted in Figure 4. To depict the relations between Internalizing and Externalizing scores independently of the magnitude of the scores, Figure 4 shows the mean differences obtained by subtracting each child's Internalizing z score from his or her Externalizing z score to obtain the E-I score. This shows that Externalizing problems predominated in referred and nonreferred boys to a greater extent than in girls at all ages. Furthermore, there was a general decline with age in Externalizing relative to Internalizing problems in all groups. Yet, referred boys continued to obtain higher Externalizing than Internalizing scores at all ages. Referred girls, by contrast, obtained higher Internalizing than Externalizing scores starting at ages 8–9, and this pattern became increasingly pronounced through age 16.

The patterns evident in Figure 4 suggest that the biological and/or environmental factors leading to differing tendencies toward Externalizing versus Internalizing problems in boys versus girls and in younger versus older children are exacerbated in those children considered deviant enough to be referred for mental health services. There were also very small tendencies (less than 1% of the variance) for referred children in the North Central and Southern regions, lower-SES children, and black children to have somewhat higher E-I scores, as compared to other children.

SUMMARY OF ACQ FINDINGS ON COMPETENCIES

As shown in Table 6, referred children obtained significantly lower scores on 20 of the 23 competence items, three competence scales, and total competence scores. Clinical status showed large effects on the School scale (25% of variance), the open-ended item for reporting additional school problems (23%), the Social scale (16%), item *VIIA. Academic performance* (17%), and total competence (17%). Medium effects were found on *VIC. Behavior with parents* (12%), *VIB. Get along with other children* (11%), *VID. Work alone* (9%), *VA. Number of friends* (9%), *VIIB. (No) Special class* (7%), and *VIA. Behavior with siblings* (6%).

Although there were 17 significant sex differences, the largest were 2% effects on *VIID. (No) School problems* (girls higher) and the School scale (girls higher).

Several age effects were larger than any of the sex effects, including a 7% effect on *IIIA. Number of jobs* (older children higher), a 6% effect on *IVA. Number of organizations* (older higher), and 5% effects on *IA. Number of sports* (nonlinear) and *IIA. Number of activities* (younger higher).

As with the problem scores, nearly all the SES effects on competence scores reflected more favorable ratings for upper-SES than lower-SES children. Some of these effects were larger than any of the SES effects on problem scores, including 5% effects for total competence and *IVA. Number of organizations* and 3% effects for *IVB. Participation in organizations, VIIA. Academic performance, VIIC. Grade repetition,* the Activities scale, and the Social scale.

Furthermore, unlike the findings for problem scores, SES effects were larger in several of the ANCOVAs of competencies among nonreferred children than in the ANCOVAs that included referred children. This suggests that the types of competencies assessed by the ACQ are positively associated with SES in the general population but less so among children who are referred for mental health services, probably because they tend to be uniformly rather low despite differences in SES backgrounds. In the ANCOVAs of the nonreferred sample and both samples together, some of the Activities items and the Activities scale score showed larger effects of region than did any problem item, the largest of which accounted for only 1% of variance. The biggest regional difference in competence scores accounted for 4% of the variance in the Activities scale for the nonreferred sample, where children in the West scored significantly higher than children in the other regions. The finding of slightly larger regional effects on Activities scores than on problem scores indicates more regional variation in the number of reported activities than in problems, although even the largest regional differences were small. Regional differences showed minimal interactions with referral status and no more than chance interactions with sex and age.

The covariate of black versus other ethnic groups showed little more than chance associations with competence scores. The covariate of non-Hispanic white versus other ethnic groups showed very small tendencies (all 1% or less of variance) for non-Hispanic white children to be scored slightly more favorably.

As with the problem scores, our finding that nonreferred children obtained significantly more favorable competence scores than referred children assessed in the survey, as well as those assessed in clinical settings, indicated that the effects associated with clinical status were not artifacts of the survey versus clinical context. Comparisons of Dutch CBCL competence scores for a nonreferred survey sample versus referred survey and clinical samples showed similar results (F. C. Verhulst, personal communication, June 17, 1988).

Sex, age, and clinical status patterns in competence scale scores.—Figures 5 and 6 depict mean Activities, Social, School, and total competence scores for children grouped by sex, age, and clinical status. The curvilinear age effect that is evident for the Activities scale accounted for the most variance (3%), with 6–11-year-olds obtaining higher scores than the younger or older groups. The main effect for clinical status and the interaction of age and clinical status both accounted for less than 1% of the variance, with nonreferred children outscoring referred children mainly at the older ages. The interaction of sex and age also accounted for less than 1% of the variance, with girls slightly outscoring boys at younger ages but the reverse occurring at older ages.

As shown in Figures 5 and 6, the Social, School, and total competence scores were all consistently lower for referred than nonreferred children of both sexes at all ages. Older children scored higher than younger children on the Social scale (2% of variance), while a tendency toward the opposite pattern on the School scale (less than 1% of variance) was accounted for mainly by the poor school performance of the older referred boys. Both referred and nonreferred girls scored better than their counterpart groups of boys on the School scale (2% of variance). This contributed to the small tendency for girls to obtain higher total competence scores (less than 1% of variance), as shown in Figure 6.

V. COMPARISON WITH PREVIOUS CBCL FINDINGS

The most similar previous research was a comparison of 1,300 referred and 1,300 nonreferred 4–16-year-olds on the CBCL (Achenbach & Edelbrock, 1981). The general design of that study was similar to the present one, although the referred sample was drawn from 28 clinical services in the eastern United States and the nonreferred sample was drawn from Washington, DC, Maryland, and northern Virginia. The CBCL survey was conducted from September through December 1976, while the CBCLs for referred children were obtained from 1974 through 1978.

The CBCL has slightly less differentiated versions of the ACQ competence items and has 118 specific problem items, plus two open-ended items for adding physical problems without known medical cause and other problems not specifically listed. The response scale for scoring problem items on the CBCL has three steps defined as 0 for "not true" of the child, 1 for "somewhat or sometimes true," and 2 for "very true or often true." Ratings are based on the preceding 6 months rather than the 2 months specified on the ACQ.

The ACQ has counterparts of 115 of the CBCL's problem items plus the open-ended item for additional problems. Some of the CBCL's problem items were split into two items on the ACQ. For example, CBCL item *43. Lying or cheating* was split into ACQ items *26. Cheats* and *101. Lies*. To make these ACQ and CBCL items comparable for purposes of analysis, we used the higher of the two scores obtained by a child on the pair of ACQ items corresponding to a single CBCL item.

CORRELATIONS BETWEEN ACQ AND CBCL ITEM SCORES

The scores obtained on the three-step CBCL response scales cannot be directly compared to the scores obtained on the four-step ACQ response scales with respect to absolute magnitude, but other types of comparisons are possible. For example, we compared the rank ordering of mean item scores obtained in the 1986 ACQ survey sample with those obtained for the 115 counterpart problem items in the 1976 CBCL survey sample by computing the r between the mean scores obtained for each of the 115 items on the ACQ and the mean scores obtained for each of the 115 items on the CBCL. To make a similar comparison for referred children, we also computed the r between mean scores for the 115 items in our current ACQ clinical sample ($N = 2,600$) and the mean scores for each of the 115 items in the CBCL clinical sample ($N = 1,300$) that was matched to the 1976 CBCL survey sample. The r of .92 between item scores in the ACQ versus CBCL survey samples and r of .95 between item scores in the ACQ versus CBCL clinical samples (both $p < .0001$) indicated great similarity between the rank ordering of item scores, despite some differences in item wording, the different response scales, the national versus regional sample, and the time elapsing between the collection of CBCL versus ACQ data. It is thus clear that there was great stability in the rank ordering of problems reported by parents of normative and referred samples of American children over the decade from 1976 to 1986.

Correlations of the mean ACQ item scores and the CBCL scores obtained from the greater Washington, DC, sample in 1976 with scores obtained by nonreferred samples during the 1980s in Holland, Puerto Rico, Thailand, and Sydney, Australia, also showed considerable cross-cultural similarity in the rank ordering of items. As summarized in Table 7, r's ranged from .69 for Holland versus Thailand to .92 for the DC area versus Sydney and for the ACQ versus the CBCL. The overall mean r was .82, computed by Fisher's z transformation. This does not necessarily mean that the absolute magnitudes of the scores were similar in all samples. The mean CBCL total problem scores were nearly identical between the DC area and Dutch samples, however, and only about 3 points higher in the Thai sample. The mean CBCL scores were higher in the Puerto Rican and Sydney samples, but the high correlations indicate that the rank orders of item scores even in these samples were very similar to those in the other samples.

COMPARISONS OF ACQ AND CBCL EFFECT SIZES FOR PROBLEM SCORES

ANCOVAs of problem scores like those summarized for the ACQ in Appendix G were also used to compare the 1976 CBCL survey and clinical samples (Achenbach & Edelbrock, 1981, table 1). The only differences in the ANCOVA designs were that the CBCL design did not include region because all data came from the eastern United States and that the CBCL covariate for ethnicity compared only black versus white groups because there were not enough children of other ethnic groups for inclusion in

TABLE 7

PEARSON r's BETWEEN MEAN SCORES FOR 115 CBCL ITEMS
AND THEIR ACQ COUNTERPARTS

Sample	ACQ	DC Area	Holland	Puerto Rico	Sydney
CBCL DC area[a]	.92				
Holland[b]	.84	.86			
Puerto Rico[c]	.84	.77	.79		
Sydney[d]	.89	.92	.81	.79	
Thailand[e]	.72	.73	.69	.73	.70

NOTE.—The correlations are between the mean scores obtained by all subjects on each of the 115 items in one sample and the mean scores obtained by all subjects on each item in all the other samples. All r's are significant at $p <$ .01. Mean r = .82 for the entire table, computed by z transformation.

[a] Achenbach & Edelbrock (1981).

[b] Achenbach, Verhulst, Baron, & Akkerhuis (1987).

[c] Achenbach, Bird, et al. (1990).

[d] Achenbach, Hensley, Phares, & Grayson (1990).

[e] Ages 6–11 only (Weisz et al., 1987).

the analyses. Because the CBCL syndromes developed at that time varied considerably among sex/age groups, they do not offer a firm basis for comparison with the current ACQ syndromes.

Of the eight ACQ items that showed large effects of clinical status, four had clear-cut counterparts on the CBCL. On the CBCL, all four of these items showed larger effects of clinical status than on the ACQ, as follows: *20. Can't concentrate,* 26% on CBCL versus 18% on ACQ; *50. Disobedient at home,* 27% versus 15%; *125. Poor school work,* 27% versus 19%; and *141. Sad or depressed,* 29% versus 15%.

Clinical status showed large effects on 30 of the 115 CBCL problem items that had ACQ counterparts, compared to only four of the 115 ACQ versions and eight of all 216 ACQ items. Furthermore, the total CBCL problem score showed a 44% effect of clinical status, compared to 22% for the total ACQ score. Although the ACQ discriminated very well between referred and nonreferred children, the variance accounted for by clinical status was thus smaller than in similar analyses of the CBCL. Possible explanations and implications will be addressed later.

Demographic effects were generally similar on the ACQ and CBCL, with negligible effects of ethnicity on specific problems and on the ACQ total problem score. There was a tendency for lower-SES children to obtain slightly higher scores on specific problems (42% of the CBCL items, 54% of the ACQ items) and on the total score, an effect accounting for less than 1% of variance on both instruments.

Age showed significant effects on many items in both instruments, with some items reflecting higher scores for older children, some for younger children, and some nonlinear age trends. Age did not have a significant effect on the ACQ total problem score, but younger children tended to obtain slightly higher total scores on the CBCL, an effect accounting for less than 1% of the variance. On both instruments, *Whining* showed the strongest tendency to be scored higher for younger children (15% on the CBCL, 13% on the ACQ). Delinquent kinds of behavior showed the strongest tendencies to be scored higher for older children, such as *Truancy* (10% on the CBCL, 8% on the ACQ) and *Uses alcohol or drugs* (13% on the CBCL, 8% for alcohol on the ACQ, 4% for drugs on the ACQ).

Significant sex differences were less numerous than age differences on both instruments. On the CBCL, girls and boys did not differ significantly in the number of items on which they scored higher (26 vs. 25) or in total score. On the ACQ, however, boys scored significantly higher than girls on significantly more items (84 vs. 46), Externalizing, and the total score (1% of variance). The higher scores for boys on more items and the total score probably reflect the larger proportion of Externalizing items on the ACQ than on the CBCL.

EFFECTS OF THE FOUR-STEP ACQ RESPONSE SCALE FOR PROBLEM SCORES

To compare the effects of the three-step CBCL versus the four-step ACQ response scales on the problem scores, we computed the ratio of the mean problem score derived from the 115 CBCL items to the mean problem score derived from the corresponding ACQ items. We did this to compare the obtained ratio with the ratio of .67 that would be expected from the difference between the 0-1-2 CBCL scale and the 0-1-2-3 ACQ scale. Because the maximum score is 2 on the CBCL scale and 3 on the ACQ scale, the ratio of obtained scores should be $(2/3 =)$ .67. Because the effect of the scale change might differ for nonreferred versus referred children, we computed the ratio separately for the CBCL survey versus ACQ survey samples and the CBCL clinical versus ACQ clinical samples.

The ratio of the mean problem scores for the CBCL versus ACQ survey samples was (CBCL/ACQ = 19.4/34.6 =) .56, whereas the ratio for the clinical samples was (56.7/74.8 =) .76. These ratios deviate in opposite directions from the .67 ratio between the maximum score of 2 obtainable on CBCL items and 3 obtainable on ACQ items. The .56 ratio obtained for the survey samples indicates that ACQ scores for nonreferred children tended to be *higher* than expected from the .67 ratio of the CBCL/ACQ response scales. By contrast, the .76 ratio obtained for the clinical samples indicates that ACQ scores for referred children tended to be *lower* than expected from the .67 ratio of the CBCL/ACQ response scales. In other words, the mean problem score on the 115 counterpart items in the ACQ survey sample should be about 29.0 (instead of the obtained $M = 34.6$) to produce a

.67 ratio in relation to the mean problem score of 19.4 obtained in the CBCL survey. Conversely, the mean problem score in the ACQ clinical sample should be about 84.6 (instead of the obtained $M = 74.8$) to produce a .67 ratio in relation to the mean problem score of 56.7 obtained in the CBCL clinical sample.

Use of the bottom step.—The fact that the mean problem score in the ACQ survey sample was actually 34.6 rather than 29.0 suggests that the four-step scale raised scores for nonreferred children by about 15.2 points rather than the 9.6 points expected from the ratio of the scales. This may have occurred because the ACQ definition of the 0 point as "never or not at all true" led a disproportionate number of parents of normal children to score relatively trivial problems as present. Such an effect was demonstrated in an experimental comparison of Canadian parents' responses to CBCL items using the standard definition of 0 as "not true" versus "never or not true" (Woodward, Thomas, Boyle, Links, & Offord, 1989). The parents receiving the "never" version scored their children significantly *higher* than the parents receiving the standard CBCL instructions without "never." The increased scores primarily reflected more frequent use of the step scored 1 on the response scale that defined the 0 point as "never." This indicates that parents tend to avoid claiming that particular problems are never true of their child.

The tendency to use the bottom step (scored 0) less often on the ACQ than on the CBCL was especially pronounced in the nonreferred samples, where chi squares showed that the bottom step of the scale was used significantly ($p < .05$) less often on 87 items of the ACQ, compared to five items of the CBCL. In the referred sample, the difference was smaller, where chi squares showed that the bottom step was used significantly less often on 52 ACQ items, compared to 14 CBCL items. The ratios 87:5 and 52:14 were both significant at $p < .001$ by binomial tests. The four-step ACQ scale thus led parents of both referred and nonreferred children to use the bottom step of the response scale less often than on the CBCL.

Use of the top step.—Our finding that the ACQ clinical sample had a mean problem score of 74.8—rather than the 84.6 expected from the ratio of the CBCL to the ACQ response scale—indicates that the four-step response scale raised scores only about 18.1 points rather than the expected 27.9 points. This may reflect the tendency of fewer parents of referred children to use the topmost step (3 = "very often or very much") when the second highest ACQ step already designated a fairly extreme degree of the problem (2 = "quite often or quite a lot"). To examine this possibility, we compared the proportion of subjects who received the topmost score on the 115 counterpart items in the ACQ and CBCL clinical samples. Chi squares showed that the topmost step was used significantly ($p < .05$) less often on

93 of the 115 counterpart items in the ACQ sample than in the CBCL sample. By contrast, the topmost step was not used significantly less often on any item in the CBCL sample than in the ACQ sample ($p < .001$ for binomial test of the ratio 93:0). It is thus clear that the change from a three-step to a four-step scale reduced use of the topmost step by parents of referred children.

There was also a tendency for parents of nonreferred children to use the topmost step less often on the ACQ than on the CBCL, but this tendency was significant on less than half as many items as in the referred samples. Chi squares showed that the top step was used significantly less often on 40 items of the ACQ versus five items of the CBCL ($p < .001$ by binomial test).

Joint effects of the differential response tendencies.—Avoidance of the bottom step of the ACQ was greatest in the nonreferred sample, whereas avoidance of the top step was greatest in the referred sample. This differential compression of scores toward the middle of the response scale in the nonreferred versus referred samples was evidently responsible for the smaller ratio of problem scores obtained by referred versus nonreferred children on the ACQ than on the CBCL. The mean problem score for referred children was 2.1 times as large as for nonreferred children on the ACQ. This contrasted with a mean problem score for referred children that was 2.9 times the mean for nonreferred children on the CBCL. For the 115 CBCL items that had counterparts on the ACQ, the ratio was also 2.9 in the original CBCL sample, compared to 2.2 for the counterpart items in the ACQ sample.

Dichotomous scoring.—In a further effort to assess the effect of the four-step response scale, we compared the percentage of variance in total problem scores accounted for by clinical status when the CBCL counterpart items on the ACQ were scored dichotomously as absent versus present according to two different cut points: (*a*) scores of 0 = "absent," while scores of 1, 2, and 3 = "present"; (*b*) scores of 0 and 1 = "absent," while scores of 2 and 3 = "present." To compare the effects of these two dichotomies on total problem scores, we performed 2 (clinical status) × 2 (sex) × 7 (age) × 4 (region) ANCOVAs with SES, non-Hispanic white, and black as covariates. Clinical status accounted for 17.3% of the variance when scores of 1, 2, and 3 = "present," compared to 22.6% of the variance when scores of 2 and 3 = "present." Counting a score of 1 as "present" thus yielded less discrimination between referred and nonreferred children than when a score of 1 was included in the "absent" category. Compared to the 0-1-2-3 scoring, where clinical status showed a 21.7% effect (Table 4), counting scores of 1 as "absent" improved discrimination somewhat, whereas counting scores of 1 as "present" reduced discrimination.

For the sake of comparison with the CBCL, an ANCOVA of the original CBCL samples scored 0 = "absent" versus 1 and 2 = "present" showed a 40.6% effect of clinical status. This was much better than the 17.3% and 22.6% effects obtained for dichotomous scoring of the ACQ items. On the other hand, it was less than the 44% effect of clinical status obtained with the 0-1-2 scoring of the CBCL. In other words, the addition of the distinction between "never" and "once in a while or just a little" on the ACQ seems to have reduced discrimination between referred and nonreferred children as compared to the three-step CBCL scale. Collapsing the ACQ's 0 and 1 steps into an "absent" category improved discrimination somewhat but still did not discriminate as well as the CBCL scale in either its three-step or collapsed 0 = "absent" versus 2 and 3 = "present" form. This suggests that encouraging parents to report very mild problems adds "noise" rather than valid variance to the identification of clinically significant deviance.

Vulnerability to respondent characteristics.—Besides raising scores among nonreferred children and reducing scores among referred children, the four-step scale may also be more vulnerable to respondent characteristics than is the three-step scale. This was suggested by the proportionately bigger differences between mean total problem scores for Time 1 versus Time 2 in the test-retest reliability sample and between mothers and fathers in the interparent agreement sample for the ACQ than were found for the CBCL (Achenbach & Edelbrock, 1983).

On the ACQ, there was a 21.5% decline from the mean Time 1 to Time 2 test-retest reliability scores, which accounted for 13.3% of the variance. On the CBCL, by contrast, there was a 9.9% decline from Time 1 to Time 2, which accounted for 3.4% of the variance. Similarly, on the ACQ, there was an 11.2% difference between the mean scores obtained from mothers and fathers rating the same referred child, which accounted for 2.2% of the variance. On the CBCL, by contrast, the difference between mothers' and fathers' mean scores for referred children was 8.7%, which accounted for only 1.2% of the variance. However, the lack of significant differences between problem scores on ACQs completed by mothers and fathers of demographically matched children in both the referred and the nonreferred samples indicates that the sex of the parent did not significantly affect the overall prevalence rates obtained for these samples. The sex of the parent was not likely to affect our comparisons between the referred and the nonreferred samples either because the samples were matched quite closely for informants. Although mothers may have a tendency to report somewhat more problems than fathers, this tendency may reach statistical significance only when both parents are involved in a clinical evaluation of their child. When fathers serve as the primary informant, their scores do not appear to differ significantly from those of mothers who serve as the primary informant.

COMPARISONS OF ACQ AND CBCL EFFECT SIZES
FOR COMPETENCE SCORES

The overall pattern of effects on ACQ competence items was similar to that found for CBCL competence items, with the largest effects being for clinical status, smaller effects for age and SES, and very small effects for sex. On the CBCL, all effects of clinical status favored nonreferred children, but two very small effects on the ACQ favored referred children, for whom significantly more sports and nonsports activities were reported. As with the problem items, the effects of clinical status were smaller on the ACQ than on the CBCL competence items. On both instruments, the open-ended item for reporting school problems showed the largest effect of any single item, but clinical status accounted for 34% of its variance on the CBCL, compared to 23% on the ACQ. The next largest effects on the competence items of both instruments were for academic performance, behavior with parents, and behavior with other children. Clinical status showed effects accounting for 21%, 22%, and 17% of the variance in these items on the CBCL, compared with 17%, 12%, and 11%, respectively, on the ACQ. Similarly, the CBCL scale scores and total competence scores discriminated more strongly between referred and nonreferred children than the ACQ scores did. The effect sizes were as follows: *Activities scale,* 11% for the CBCL versus less than 1% for the ACQ; *Social scale,* 28% versus 16%; *School scale,* 30% versus 25%; and *total competence,* 35% versus 17% (inclusion of the ACQ open-ended items for the best things and greatest concerns about your child—which are not on the CBCL—raised the effect size on total competence from 17% to 18%).

VI. DISCRIMINATION BETWEEN THE NORMAL AND THE CLINICAL RANGE

Criteria are often sought for discriminating between individuals who are relatively normal and those who are clinically deviant. Improving the accuracy of such discrimination is important for identifying individuals who may need special help even though they have not been referred and for making appropriate diagnostic decisions about individuals who are referred for help. One way to obtain discriminating criteria is by identifying cut points on distributions of scores that maximize the accuracy with which individuals are classified into the normal versus clinical range. We identified cut points by comparing the distributions of total problem and competence scores for our referred versus nonreferred samples. To take account of possible sex and age differences, we did this separately for each sex at ages 4–5, 6–11, and 12–16.

PROBLEM SCORES

On the distribution of total problem scores for each sex in each age range, we identified the score that minimized the sum of "false positives" (the percentage of nonreferred children who scored above the cut point) and "false negatives" (the percentage of referred children who scored below the cut point). These variables are often stated in reverse fashion as one minus false positives equals true negatives, or *specificity*, and one minus false negatives equals true positives, or *sensitivity*. To provide uniform standards for comparison across groups, we also computed the false positives and false negatives obtained by using cut points as close as possible to the 80th and 90th percentiles of the nonreferred samples. For each of these two cut points, we computed the mean of the false positives and false negatives across all the sex/age groups to obtain the overall misclassification rate.

Referral for mental health services is, of course, not an infallible criterion for identifying "true positives." Some nonreferred children in our sample may have needed help but were not referred or would, in fact, be referred soon after the survey. Some referred children, on the other hand, may not have needed referral but had parents who were overly concerned about their child's behavior or who were seeking help for themselves. However, as reviewed previously (Achenbach & Edelbrock, 1981), other criteria for defining true positives in large surveys—such as direct clinical assessment and clinicians' judgments of interview data—have proved to be even more fallible than actual referral (e.g., Langner et al., 1976). Thus, although use of any fallible criterion may underestimate the accuracy with which measures such as the ACQ classify children as being in the clinical versus normal range, actual referral within the preceding 12 months is likely to be as good as any criterion currently applicable to large surveys.

The most efficient cut points (i.e., those that minimized the sum of false positives and false negatives) ranged from the 80th percentile for girls 6–11 to the 85th percentile for boys 6–11. Using the most efficient cut points for each group, the mean misclassification rate across all groups was 26.7%. This mean misclassification rate was computed by averaging the percentage of false positives plus false negatives across referred and nonreferred samples from the six sex/age groups. Using a uniform 80th percentile cut point, the mean misclassification rate was 27.7%. And using a uniform 90th percentile cut point, the misclassification rate was 29.0%. On both the ACQ and the CBCL, the total misclassification rates remained fairly constant for cut points between the 80th and the 90th percentiles. For practical applications of the CBCL, Achenbach and Edelbrock (1981) selected the 90th percentile, which produced an overall mean misclassification rate of 17.6% for the CBCL. The CBCL misclassification rate of 17.6% thus indicated better discrimination by the CBCL than the minimum misclassification rate of 26.7% found for the ACQ, probably owing to the better performance of the CBCL's three-step response scale discussed previously.

To test the 80th percentile ACQ cut point for children who were all assessed in the survey context, we assessed the cut point's effectiveness for discriminating between the 88 demographically matched referred and non-referred survey children. In this group of 176 children, 38.6% of those who had been referred in the previous 12 months scored below the cut point, while 20.5% of those who had not been referred scored above the cut point. Even though the referred children might have improved since their referral, the overall misclassification rate of ([38.6% + 20.5%]/2 =) 29.6% was less than 2% above the rate of 27.7% obtained for children assessed at referral versus nonreferred children. A 2×2 $\chi^2 = 30.46$, $p < .001$, showed a highly significant association between the cut point and referral status in the survey sample. The relative risk odds ratio (Fleiss, 1981) showed that children referred in the previous 12 months were 6.18 times more likely to exceed the cut point than children who had not been referred (99% confidence interval = 2.55–14.95). The 80th percentile cut point thus worked well in discriminating between previously referred and nonreferred children in the survey context as well as when referred children were assessed at intake into mental health services.

Because it is unlikely that all children truly fall into the two mutually exclusive categories "normal" and "deviant," it is often desirable to use an intermediate or borderline category. To portray relations between referral status and cut points in a more differentiated fashion, Table 8 shows the mean percentage of children (averaged over the six sex/age groups) who would be classified according to a cut point at the 80th percentile for the upper limit of the normal range, between the 81st and the 90th percentile for the borderline abnormal range, and above the 90th percentile for the clinical range. Using this tripartite division, the mean of the misclassification rate of false positives (nonreferred who scored above the 90th percentile) and false negatives (referred who scored at or under the 80th percentile) would be 22.7%. That is, the 10.2% false positive rate obtained for the nonreferred sample and the 35.2% false negative rate obtained for the referred sample averaged to 22.7% total misclassifications. The 9.8% of the nonreferred sample and 12.6% of the referred sample scoring between the 81st and the 90th percentiles averaged to 11.2% being classified as borderline.

COMPETENCE SCORES

To identify cut points on the total competence scores, we followed a procedure like that used for the total problem scores. However, because the competence scores for referred children are generally *lower* than those for nonreferred children, the best cut points are at relatively low competence scores, with the clinical range being below the cut point and the normal range being above the cut point.

The cut points that minimized the misclassification rate ranged from

TABLE 8

PERCENTAGE OF CHILDREN CLASSIFIED ACCORDING TO THREE CATEGORIES OF
TOTAL PROBLEM SCORES

	Nonreferred Sample	Referred Sample
1. Above the 90th percentile	False positive = 10.2	True positive = 52.4
2. From the 81st to the 90th percentile	Borderline = 9.8	Borderline = 12.6
3. At or below the 90th percentile	True negative = 80.0	False negative = 35.2

the 21st percentile for boys aged 6–11 and girls aged 12–16 to the 27th percentile for girls aged 6–11. The mean misclassification rate using these cut points was 36.3%. Using a uniform 20th percentile cut point for comparability with the 80th percentile cut point for the ACQ problem scores, the mean misclassification rate was 37.0%. Cut points below the 20th percentile generally produced higher misclassification rates because of the increase in false negatives. All the ACQ cut points thus produced higher misclassification rates than the 25.9% rate obtained with the 10th percentile cut point on the CBCL competence scores.

COMBINED PROBLEM AND COMPETENCE CUT POINTS

To test the discriminative accuracy of the combined cut points for competence and problems, we divided our sample of 5,200 referred and nonreferred children into the following four categories:

1. *Deviant on both scores.*—Children scoring above the 80th percentile cut point on the problem scores and at or below the 20th percentile cut point on the competence scores;
2. *Deviant on the problem score but not the competence score.*—Children scoring above the 80th percentile on the problem score but above the 20th percentile on the competence score;
3. *Deviant on the competence score but not the problem score.*—Children scoring at or below the 20th percentile on the competence score but at or below the 80th percentile on the problem score; and
4. *Not deviant on either score.*—Children scoring at or below the 80th percentile on the problem score and above the 20th percentile on the competence score.

Table 9 summarizes the classification of referred and nonreferred children into the four categories described above. If we consider only the children who were deviant on both the problem and the competence scores and the children who were not deviant on either score (categories 1 and 4), the misclassification rate fell to 5.2% false positives and 23.4% false negatives. Averaging the 5.2% false positives from the nonreferred sample and 23.4% false negatives from the referred sample produced a mean misclassification rate of 14.3%, compared to the 27.7% rate obtained with the problem cut point alone and the 37.0% rate obtained with the competence cut point alone. However, 33.5% of the children fell into the mixed categories 2 and 3; that is, they were within the normal range on one score but not the other.

To test the effects of dividing the mixed categories 2 and 3 in different ways, we first added both mixed categories 2 and 3 to the uniformly deviant

TABLE 9

Percentage of Children Classified according to 80th Percentile Cutoff on Problem Score and 20th Percentile Cutoff on Competence Score

Group	Problems	Competence	Sample	
			Nonreferred	Referred
1. Deviant on both scores	> 80th	≤ 20th	False positive = 5.2	True positive = 37.8
2. Deviant only on problem score ...	> 80th	> 20th	Mixed = 14.6	Mixed = 27.4
3. Deviant only on competence score ...	≤ 80th	≤ 20th	Mixed = 13.6	Mixed = 11.4
4. Not deviant on either score	≤ 80th	> 20th	True negative = 66.5	False negative = 23.4

category 1 to define the deviant group. This produced a misclassification rate of 33.4% for the nonreferred sample and 23.4% for the referred sample, for an overall misclassification rate of 28.4%.

We then added the two mixed categories (2 and 3) to the uniformly nondeviant category (4) to define the nondeviant group. This produced a misclassification rate of 5.2% for the nonreferred group and 62.2% for the referred group, for an overall misclassification rate of 33.7%. It thus appears that, when using both the competence and the problem scores, it is preferable to consider deviance on *either* the competence or the problem score as a basis for classifying a child as deviant (28.4% misclassification when both mixed categories were classified as deviant vs. 33.7% when both were classified as nondeviant). The overall misclassification rate of 27.7% using the 80th percentile cut point on the problem score alone, however, was slightly better than the 28.4% misclassification obtained using the combined problem and competence score cut points with mixed cases classified as deviant. Nevertheless, if we allow a mixed group of 33.5% who are deviant on one scale but not the other, the misclassification rate can be reduced to 5.2% false positives and 23.4% false negatives, for a mean misclassification rate of 14.3%.

For the sake of comparison, the CBCL misclassification rate based on the joint use of problem and competence scores was 2% false positives and 16% false negatives, for a mean misclassification rate of 9%, with 26.8% in the mixed category of being deviant on one score but not the other. Omitting the mixed category, the false positive rates translate into specificities of 94.8% for the ACQ and 98% for the CBCL. The false negative rates translate into sensitivities of 76.6% for the ACQ and 84% for the CBCL.

SUMMARY OF CATEGORICAL CUT POINTS

The findings from both the ACQ and the CBCL agree in showing that false positives and negatives can be minimized by identifying a mixed group of children who are in the clinical range on only the competence or the problem score. This procedure produced very low false positive rates on both instruments (5.4% on the ACQ, 2% on the CBCL) and moderate false negative rates (23.2% on the ACQ, 16% on the CBCL). The resulting mean misclassification rates were 14.3% on the ACQ and 9% on the CBCL, with 33.4% classified as borderline on the ACQ and 26.8% on the CBCL. A simpler procedure that produces a smaller mixed (or borderline) group is to divide the ACQ problem scores into those at or below the 80th percentile, those between the 81st and the 90th percentile, and those above the 90th percentile. This procedure produced 10.2% false positives, 35.2% false negatives, 22.8% total misclassifications, and 11.2% in the borderline group.

No matter what diagnostic or classification criterion is used, cases that are on the border between the normal and the clinical ranges are difficult to classify reliably as normal versus clinical (e.g., Robins, 1985). Rather than trying to force such cases into the normal versus clinical category, it may therefore be preferable to identify them explicitly. This would facilitate recognition of their potential differences from cases that are clearly in the normal range and those that are clearly in the clinical range.

When parents' ratings are used for screening purposes, cases found to be borderline would be key candidates for further screening by procedures other than parents' ratings in order to determine whether the cases could be more decisively placed into the normal or clinical range. On the other hand, even extensive multimethod assessments may identify some children as being truly in the border region between the normal range, where no professional help is warranted, and the clinical range, where most people would agree that help is needed.

For research purposes, forcing borderline cases into one extreme category or the other may cause us to underestimate the discriminative accuracy that can be attained with the cases that can be clearly classified as normal versus clinical. For clinical purposes, classification of borderline cases as normal could deny some children the extra attention they would get if they were recognized as not clearly in the normal range. Classification of borderline cases as deviant, on the other hand, could result in more intensive or stigmatizing interventions than are warranted.

When discriminating between the normal and the clinical ranges on the basis of a single instrument, it is highly desirable to use a borderline category for children whose scores do not clearly place them in the normal or the clinical range. As detailed elsewhere (Achenbach, 1991a), borderline categories can also be helpful when defined in terms of differences between scores obtained from different sources of data, such as parents, teachers, self-reports, interviews, direct observations, and tests.

The important point is that our evaluation of assessment and taxonomic procedures should not be locked into an unrealistically simplistic "sick-versus-well" decision model. Such a model misrepresents the kinds of decisions that would be most helpful and may underestimate the ability of assessment procedures to aid in making realistically flexible decisions.

DISCRIMINANT ANALYSES

Total problem and competence scores.—To determine whether differential weighting of problem and competence scores could improve discrimination between referred and nonreferred children, we computed discriminant functions in which the total problem and total competence scores were both entered as predictors of outcome groups classified as referred versus nonreferred. Because discriminant analysis optimally weights predictors to maximize their joint association with the classification of outcomes within a particular sample, the results must be cross-validated by applying the weights derived in one sample to prediction of the outcome variable in another sample. For comparability with the CBCL discriminant analyses (Achenbach & Edelbrock, 1981), we did this by dividing our referred and nonreferred samples in half in order to compute a discriminant function on one half and cross-validate it on the other half.

Using half the referred and nonreferred subjects, we computed separate discriminant functions for each sex at ages 4–5, 6–11, and 12–16. We then applied the weights for the problem and competence scores obtained from these discriminant functions to the other half of each sex/age sample and computed the mean of the false positives and false negatives for each sex/age group. (N for initial and cross-validation samples of each sex was 200 at ages 4–5, 600 at ages 6–11, and 500 at ages 12–16.)

Based on the weighted combination of problem and competence scores, the cross-validated misclassification rate ranged from a low of 20.1% for boys aged 12–16 to a high of 29.5% for girls aged 4–5. The mean misclassification rate computed by averaging the rates across the six sex/age groups was 26.2%, with a specificity of 84.8% and a sensitivity of 62.8%. The misclassification rate was thus only slightly better than the mean 27.7% rate obtained by using the 80th percentile cut point on problem scores and the 26.7% rate obtained by using the most efficient cut points for each sex/age group. It is somewhat better than the 28.6% misclassification rate obtained when the unweighted competence and problem scores were used to classify subjects as normal if both scores were in the normal range and deviant if at least one of the scores was in the clinical range.

The addition of the total competence score thus reduced misclassifications 1.5%, to 26.2% from the 27.7% obtained with the 80th percentile problem score cut point alone, but only when the competence score was differentially weighted via discriminant functions. On the CBCL, however, the addition of the total competence score improved the discrimination obtained with the 90th percentile problem score by about 2% whether the discriminant weights (15.4% misclassification) or unweighted percentile cut points (15.5% misclassification) were used.

Syndrome and competence scales.—As another way of testing the effect of differential weighting, we computed stepwise discriminant functions in which each of the competence and syndrome scales were the predictors and referral status was the classification variable. A "jackknife" procedure was used whereby discriminant functions were computed and cross-validated on successive subsamples drawn from a complete sample (SAS Institute, 1988). Separate discriminant functions were computed within each of the six sex/

age groups by entering scales in the order of their reduction of Wilks's lambda in relation to the classification of children as referred versus nonreferred. The addition of scales as predictors was stopped when no more scales significantly ($p < .05$) reduced lambda.

The misclassification rates ranged from a low of 15.8% for boys aged 12–16 to a high of 27.4% for girls aged 4–5. For each sex, the misclassification rates declined with increases in age. Averaging the rates across the six sex/age groups yielded a mean misclassification rate of 20.5%, which is considerably better than the 27.2% rate obtained from the discriminant analyses of total competence and total problem scores. Specificity was 85.2%, while sensitivity was 73.7%.

Table 10 shows the percentage of variance uniquely accounted for by each scale that made a significant ($p < .05$) contribution to discrimination between referred and nonreferred children within each sex/age group. Table 10 also indicates the total percentage of variance accounted for by the combination of the significant scales for each sex/age group. According to Cohen's (1988) criteria, effects of this type that account for 2%–13% of variance are small, those accounting for 13%–26% medium, and those accounting for 26% or more large.

As can be seen from Table 10, the weighted combinations of scale scores accounted for a large percentage of variance in clinical status in

TABLE 10

PERCENTAGE OF VARIANCE ACCOUNTED FOR BY SCALES[a] THAT MADE SIGNIFICANT
($p < .05$) CONTRIBUTIONS TO DISCRIMINATION BETWEEN
REFERRED AND NONREFERRED SAMPLES

	BOYS			GIRLS		
SCALE	4–5	6–11	12–16	4–5	6–11	12–16
Activities	3	2	2	. . .	2	< 1
Social	9	2	3	4	4	2
School	NA[b]	14	42	NA[b]	26	31
Withdrawn	2	. . .	< 1	. . .	. . .	15
Somatic Complaints	. . .	. . .	. . .	. . .	. . .	1
Anxious/Depressed	. . .	< 1	13	. . .	10	2
Social Problems	2	. . .	< 1	. . .	. . .	< 1
Thought Problems	. . .	< 1	. . .	. . .	. . .	. . .
Attention Problems	24	32	2	2	< 1	1
Delinquent Behavior	. . .	1	< 1	2	< 1	1
Aggressive Behavior	. . .	. . .	. . .	20	. . .	< 1
Total percentage of variance accounted for[c]	35	45	54	26	38	47

[a] Percentage of variance is the partial r^2 of each scale with the referred-nonreferred dichotomy, after the other scales were partialed out.

[b] NA = School scale was not analyzed for ages 4–5.

[c] Total percentage of variance accounted for is R^2.

all six sex/age groups. The effect sizes ranged from 26% of variance for 4–5-year-old girls to 54% for 12–16-year-old boys. Like the accuracy of classification, the total effect sizes increased with the age of the subjects.

The School scale was a major contributor to the discrimination of clinical status for all four sex/age groups for which it is scored, with effect sizes ranging from 14% for 6–11-year-old boys to 42% for 12–16-year-old boys. The Attention Problems syndrome scale was a significant contributor to all the discriminant analyses, with the largest effects being for 4–5-year-old boys (24% of variance) and 6–11-year-old boys (32% of variance). It should be remembered, however, that collinearity among scales could have affected the ordering and magnitude of their contributions as portrayed by the discriminant analyses. Scales that made small or nonsignificant contributions to the discriminant analyses may nevertheless be strongly associated with clinical status when analyzed alone. Thus, for example, the Delinquent Behavior scale had a large association with clinical status when analyzed alone via ANCOVA (App. G) but small associations in the discriminant analyses. This is probably because scales with which it shared variance had still stronger associations and preceded it into the discriminant analyses, thereby accounting for much of the variance that the Delinquent Behavior scale would account for if it were analyzed alone. The exceptionally large associations shown by the Attention Problems and School scales are commensurate with their exceptionally large effect sizes in the ANCOVAs (App. G, Table 7). There is thus no doubt about their strong associations with clinical status.

Problem and competence items.—To test the discriminative power of weighted combinations of individual items, we first computed one set of cross-validated discriminant functions using all the ACQ problem items as candidate predictors and a second set of cross-validated discriminant functions using all the competence items as candidate predictors. After identifying the problem and competence items that separately made significant contributions to the prediction of referral status, we computed stepwise discriminant functions for each sex/age group in which both these problem and competence items served as candidate predictors. The addition of problem and competence items as predictors was stopped when no more items significantly ($p < .05$) reduced lambda.

Averaged across all six sex/age groups, the mean cross-validated misclassification rate was 14.1% for the problem items alone, 19.4% for the competence items alone, and 13.3% for the problem and competence items together. The false positive rate for the combined problem and competence items was 7.9%, while the false negative rate was 19.6%. These error rates translate into a specificity of 92.1% and sensitivity of 80.4%. Analyses omitting subjects who were in the 81st–90th percentile range for total problem scores produced similar results.

The number of problem items remaining in the discriminant functions ranged from 12 to 27, while the number of competence items ranged from four to 10 among the six sex/age groups. The total percentage of variance accounted for ranged from 55.9% for girls aged 6–11 to 62.7% for boys aged 4–5. The specific surviving items varied among the sex/age groups. The only item that made a significant contribution in all six sex/age groups was the number of nonsports activities, which tended to be scored higher in the referred than the nonreferred samples. The tendency for the number of activities to be higher among referred children on the ACQ was the *opposite* of findings with the CBCL, where nonreferred children obtained significantly higher scores (Achenbach & Edelbrock, 1981). This may reflect the larger number of entries permitted on the ACQ than the CBCL (four versus three), which might have encouraged some parents of referred children to list more activities, either because they try to involve their children in as many activities as possible or because their children indicate a liking for a greater variety of activities. However, ACQ ratings of amount and quality of participation in activities were significantly lower for referred than nonreferred children (see Table 6). Furthermore, the effect of number of activities did not exceed 4% in any sex/age group, which is at the low end of Cohen's (1988) range of 2%–13% for small effect sizes of partial r^2 in regression/discriminant analyses. Because collinearity among the candidate predictors is apt to have contributed to variations in the other predictors that survived, the consistency with which number of activities survived suggests that it represents relatively unique variance, albeit a small amount.

The second most consistently significant surviving predictor was the open-ended item concerning the best things about the child. This item was a significant predictor in the discriminant analyses for five of the six sex/age groups, with effect sizes ranging up to 4% for 4–5-year-old boys.

Among the problem items, the most consistently significant surviving predictor was *125. Poor school work,* which made significant contributions in four sex/age groups. The effects in the following three groups were much larger than for any competence items: boys 6–11, 32%; boys 12–16, 43%; and girls 6–11, 23%, where effects of 26% or more are large by Cohen's criteria. The only other items to show large effects in any sex/age group were *141. Sad or depressed,* which showed a 32% effect for girls 12–16, and *51. Disobedient at school,* which showed a 29% effect for boys 4–5.

VII. FINDINGS ON THE FAMILY INTERVIEW VARIABLES

Appendix D lists the questions about family variables that were asked following the ACQ. Because the questions were asked only in the survey sample, all analyses presented here pertain only to the survey sample.

To test relations between the ACQ and family variables, we combined the stratified nonreferred sample of 2,600, the 88 referred subjects identified in the survey, and the remaining 46 survey subjects who duplicated already filled age-sex-PSU strata without being from the same family as any other subject, for a total N of 2,734. To summarize relations between the family variables and problem scores on the ACQ, Table 11 shows the percentage of subjects categorized by each family variable who had total problem scores at or above the 80th percentile, between the 81st and the 90th percentile, and above the 90th percentile for their sex/age group. The percentages thus sum to 100 in each column of each part of the table, with some deviations due to rounding error. The chi square results shown for each item were based on the actual cell frequencies, but the data are displayed as percentages of each column to aid the reader in seeing relations between each family characteristic and the three categories of ACQ problem scores.

HOUSEHOLD COMPOSITION

Parts A–D in Table 11 summarize several aspects of household composition in relation to the classification of children according to the three categories of ACQ problem scores.

Parts A and B indicate that the number of adults in the household had *opposite* associations with problem scores, depending on whether the adults were related or unrelated to the child. Specifically, the fewer related adults in the household, the greater the prevalence of high ACQ problem scores ($p < .001$). Conversely, the more unrelated adults, the greater the prevalence of high ACQ scores ($p < .007$).

TABLE 11

PERCENTAGE OF CHILDREN CLASSIFIED BY FAMILY INTERVIEW VARIABLES AND ACQ
PROBLEM SCORES AT OR BELOW THE 80TH, FROM THE 81ST TO THE 90TH,
AND ABOVE THE 90TH PERCENTILE[a]

A. NUMBER OF ADULTS IN THE HOUSEHOLD WHO ARE RELATED TO THE SUBJECT

ACQ Percentile	1	2	3	> 3	N
≤ 80	72.3	79.3	82.6	87.6	2,148
81–90	9.7	9.9	9.3	9.3	267
> 90	18.0	10.8	8.1	3.1	313
N	494	1,847	258	129	2,728

$$\chi^2(6) = 34.19, p < .001, \phi = .11$$

NOTE.—The fewer related adults, the greater the proportion of high ACQ scores.

B. NUMBER OF ADULTS IN THE HOUSEHOLD WHO ARE NOT RELATED TO THE SUBJECT

ACQ Percentile	0	1	> 1	N
≤ 80	79.3	71.5	66.7	2,131
81–90	9.8	10.5	14.8	267
> 90	11.0	18.0	18.5	312
N	2,511	172	27	2,710

$$\chi^2(4) = 10.56, p = .032, \phi = .06$$

NOTE.—The proportion of high ACQ scores was greater in families having unrelated adults.

C. NUMBER OF CHILDREN IN THE HOUSEHOLD (Including Subject)

ACQ Percentile	1	2	3	> 3	N
≤ 80	82.2	77.9	76.4	79.6	2,144
81–90	8.1	10.6	10.6	8.8	267
> 90	9.7	11.6	13.0	11.6	315
N	566	1,079	660	421	2,726

$$\chi^2(6) = 7.50, p = .280, \phi = .05$$

NOTE.—No significant relation between number of children and high ACQ scores.

D. MARITAL STATUS OF PARENTS

ACQ Percentile	Married to Subject's Parent or Widowed	Unmarried to Subject's Parent, Separated, Divorced	N
≤ 80	81.3	72.1	2,144
81–90	9.5	10.6	267
> 90	9.2	17.4	315
N	1,958	768	2,726

$$\chi^2(2) = 38.75, p < .001, \phi = .12$$

NOTE.—The proportion of high ACQ scores was greater where parents were unmarried, separated, or divorced.

68

TABLE 11 (*Continued*)

E. Aid to Families with Dependent Children (AFDC)

ACQ Percentile	No	Yes	N
≤ 80	79.6	70.5	2,144
81–90	10.2	6.5	267
> 90	10.3	23.0	314
N	2,464	261	2,725

$$\chi^2(2) = 38.56, p < .001, \phi = .12$$

Note.—The proportion of high ACQ scores was greater in AFDC families.

F. Aid for Women, Infants, and Children (WIC)

ACQ Percentile	No	Yes	N
≤ 80	79.0	70.0	2,136
81–90	9.8	10.0	267
> 90	11.2	20.0	313
N	2,606	110	2,716

$$\chi^2(2) = 8.24, p = .016, \phi = .06$$

Note.—The proportion of high ACQ scores was greater in WIC families.

G. Food Stamps

ACQ Percentile	No	Yes	N
≤ 80	79.2	75.1	2,144
81–90	10.1	8.0	267
> 90	10.7	16.9	314
N	2,375	350	2,725

$$\chi^2(2) = 11.88, p = .003, \phi = .07$$

Note.—The proportion of high ACQ scores was greater in food stamp families.

H. Unemployment Benefits

ACQ Percentile	No	Yes	N
≤ 80	78.9	71.1	2,141
81–90	9.7	13.2	267
> 90	11.8	15.8	313
N	2,645	76	2,721

$$\chi^2(2) = 2.72, p = .26, \phi = .03$$

Note.—No significant relation between unemployment benefits and high ACQ scores.

TABLE 11 (*Continued*)

I. OTHER GOVERNMENT ASSISTANCE

ACQ Percentile	No	Yes	N
≤ 80	79.2	72.9	2,141
81–90	9.7	11.0	267
> 90	11.1	16.1	313
N	2,503	218	2,721

$$\chi^2(2) = 5.61, p = .061, \phi = .05$$

NOTE.—Borderline significant relation between other government assistance and high ACQ scores.

J. ANY FORM OF GOVERNMENT ASSISTANCE

ACQ Percentile	No	Yes	N
≤ 80	80.4	73.0	2,152
81–90	10.0	8.9	267
> 90	9.6	18.1	315
N	2,127	607	2,734

$$\chi^2(2) = 33.36, p < .001, \phi = .11$$

NOTE.—The proportion of high ACQ scores was greater in families receiving any assistance.

K. NUMBER OF HOUSEHOLD AND FAMILY MEMBERS RECEIVING MENTAL HEALTH SERVICES (Besides Subject)

ACQ Percentile	0	1	> 1	N
≤ 80	80.5	71.2	56.0	2,146
81–90	9.4	10.4	17.6	267
> 90	10.1	18.4	26.4	314
N	2,337	299	91	2,727

$$\chi^2(4) = 49.19, p < .001, \phi = .13$$

NOTE.—The more members receiving mental health services, the greater the proportion of high ACQ scores.

[a] Total N = 2,734 survey subjects, including nonreferred sample of 2,600, 46 extra subjects for already filled strata, and 88 referred subjects. N was reduced by missing or unclassifiable data for some items. Chi square analyses were based on the actual cell frequencies, but, to aid the reader, the cell frequencies are displayed in terms of the percentage of subjects in each column who were classified by each level of the variable.

In part A, 18.0% of children in homes having only one related adult scored above the 90th percentile, whereas only 10.8% of children in homes having two related adults did so. The percentage scoring above the 90th percentile continued to decline as the number of related adults increased, as 8.1% scored above the 90th percentile in homes where there were three related adults and 3.1% where there were more than three related adults. Thus, not only did the increase from one to more than one related adults appear to be beneficial, but so did a continuing increase beyond two related adults.

Yet it was not the presence of more adults per se that was beneficial because high problem scores were more prevalent in homes that included unrelated adults: 11.0% of children living with no unrelated adults scored above the 90th percentile, whereas the rate was 18.0% for children living with one unrelated adult and 18.5% for those living with more than one unrelated adult. The percentage scoring at or below the 80th percentile declined from 79.3% where there were no unrelated adults to 71.5% where there was one unrelated adult and 66.7% where there were more than one unrelated adults. The presence of unrelated adults no doubt signified a different type of family environment that could be associated with higher problem scores for a variety of reasons.

Unlike the number of adults, the number of children in the household was not significantly associated with high problem scores, as shown by part C ($p = .28$).

As part D shows, the marital status of the child's parents was significantly related to problem scores ($p < .001$). Because preliminary analyses showed similar proportions of children above the 80th percentile where the parents were either married to each other or widowed, these two categories were combined for comparison with those that involved failure to marry the parent or separation or divorce from the parent. The percentage of scores above the 90th percentile was significantly lower where the parents were married to each other or widowed (9.2%) than where the other conditions prevailed (17.4%). The percentage scoring above the 80th percentile was 23.9% where the parents had never married and were not living together, 29.7% where they were separated or divorced, and 66.7% where they were not married to each other but were living together, although this category comprised only six cases.

PUBLIC ASSISTANCE

Parts E–J in Table 11 summarize relations between various forms of public assistance and classification according to the ACQ scores. The prevalence of high ACQ scores was significantly greater for children in families receiving Aid to Families with Dependent Children (AFDC; $p < .001$), Aid for Women, Infants, and Children (WIC; $p = .016$), and food stamps ($p = .003$). There was a borderline significant association with other forms of government assistance that did not fall into the main categorical programs ($p = .061$) and no significant association with unemployment benefits ($p = .26$). Combining across all categories, children in families receiving any one or more types of assistance were significantly more likely to obtain high ACQ scores than children in families not receiving any assistance ($p < .001$).

As indicated in Table 11, the $\chi^2 = 38.56$ for AFDC showed that it was the form of assistance having the strongest association with high ACQ scores.

MENTAL HEALTH SERVICES

Part K in Table 11 shows that, the more household and family members besides the subject receiving mental health services, the greater the prevalence of high ACQ scores ($p < .001$). Not only was the overall chi square significant, but a further chi square showed a significantly greater proportion of high ACQ scores where two or more household or family members received mental health services than where only one received services, $\chi^2(2) = 7.56, p = .023, \phi = .14$.

Because interviewers also asked where the mental health services were received, we compared cases involving only outpatient services ($N = 269$) with those involving inpatient services ($N = 74$). A chi square showed no significant association between ACQ problem scores and outpatient versus inpatient services received by household and family members.

Responses to questions about diagnosis indicated that most respondents could not specify the diagnoses. However, among those that were specified, the most common were depressive disorders ($N = 60$) and anxiety disorders, including phobias ($N = 18$). A t test showed significantly higher ACQ total problem scores where depressive diagnoses were reported than in demographically matched subjects for whom no household or family mental health services were reported ($M = 81.4$ vs. $65.2, t = 1.99, p = .05$).

CHILD CARE

Besides the items listed in Table 11, we analyzed relations between classification according to the 80th percentile cut point and the child-care questions shown in Appendix D. Because age levels were likely to be related to associations with child care, we performed separate analyses for ages 4–5, 6–11, and 12–16. When we classified children according to the number of hours of care in the home, out of the home, by relatives, and by nonrelatives and also by the number of children in care together, we found few significant associations with ACQ problem scores. The few significant associations suggested that more out-of-home care by nonrelatives was associated with a greater prevalence of scores above the 80th percentile for 6–11-year-olds and that total amount of care out of the home—whether by relatives or nonrelatives—was similarly associated with a greater prevalence of scores above the 80th percentile for 12–16-year-olds. However, the associations occurred in only a relatively small proportion of the tests of child-care variables and were relatively weak.

RELATIONS OF FAMILY INTERVIEW VARIABLES TO
INTERNALIZING AND EXTERNALIZING

Total problem scores provide a global index of deviance across many areas. It is possible that some family variables are associated with a general elevation of diverse problems, whereas other family variables are associated with particular subgroups or patterns of problems. Although we plan to test the differential predictive power and other correlates of specific syndromes in subsequent studies of the current sample, such analyses are beyond the scope of the present *Monograph*. However, the division of problem items into broad-band Internalizing and Externalizing groupings enabled us to test the associations between the family variables and these contrasting types of problems.

As described in Chapter III, we derived the Internalizing and Externalizing groupings of problem items from second-order principal factor analyses of eight cross-informant syndromes (Achenbach, 1991a). Internalizing and Externalizing were scored as separate linear variables for each child. Although these two groupings are sometimes viewed as opposites, problems from both groupings often coexist in the same children. Because children who have many problems in a particular area often have elevated problems in other areas as well, positive correlations are typically found between Internalizing and Externalizing problems scored in broad samples of children (Achenbach & Edelbrock, 1983, 1986, 1987). Nevertheless, it may be clinically useful to distinguish between children who have primarily Internalizing problems and those who have primarily Externalizing problems. The situation is analogous to patterns of ability test scores, such as those found on the Wechsler Intelligence Scale for Children–Revised (WISC-R; Wechsler, 1974). Even though there is a positive correlation between verbal scores and performance scores, children who have much higher verbal than performance scores may differ in clinically important ways from children who show the opposite pattern.

To distinguish extreme groups of children who have primarily Internalizing problems from those who have primarily Externalizing problems within the survey sample of 2,734, we first converted the Internalizing scores to z scores separately for each sex within the two-year age intervals used for our ANCOVAs. We also converted the Externalizing scores to z scores within the same groups. We then subtracted each child's Internalizing score from his or her Externalizing score to obtain an E-I score. (Note that

TABLE 12

PERCENTAGE OF CHILDREN CLASSIFIED BY FAMILY INTERVIEW VARIABLES AND
EXTERNALIZING-INTERNALIZING DIFFERENCE SCORES AT OR
BELOW THE 10TH AND ABOVE THE 90TH PERCENTILE[a]

A. NUMBER OF ADULTS IN THE HOUSEHOLD WHO ARE RELATED TO THE SUBJECT

	1	2	> 2	N
Externalizers	57.5	51.6	61.5	308
Internalizers	42.5	48.4	38.5	262
N	127	378	65	570

$$\chi^2(2) = 2.99, p = .224, \phi = .07$$

NOTE.—No significant relation between number of related adults and E-I scores.

B. NUMBER OF ADULTS IN THE HOUSEHOLD WHO ARE NOT RELATED TO THE SUBJECT

	0	> 0	N
Externalizers	52.9	66.7	304
Internalizers	47.1	33.3	259
N	518	45	563

$$\chi^2(1) = 3.16, p = .075, \phi = .08$$

NOTE.—Borderline tendency for households with more unrelated adults to have greater proportion of Externalizers.

C. NUMBER OF CHILDREN IN THE HOUSEHOLD (Including Subject)

	1	2	3	> 3	N
Externalizers	52.3	53.6	52.1	59.8	308
Internalizers	47.7	46.4	47.9	40.2	262
N	109	220	144	97	570

$$\chi^2(3) = 1.66, p = .645, \phi = .05$$

NOTE.—No significant relation between number of children and E-I scores.

D. MARITAL STATUS OF PARENTS

	Married to Subject's Parent or Widowed	Unmarried to Subject's Parent, Separated, Divorced	N
Externalizers	50.4	61.5	306
Internalizers	49.6	38.5	259
N	373	192	565

$$\chi^2(1) = 6.24, p < .012, \phi = .11$$

NOTE.—The proportion of Externalizers was greater where parents were unmarried, separated, or divorced.

TABLE 12 (*Continued*)

E. Aid to Families with Dependent Children (AFDC)

	No	Yes	N
Externalizers	51.4	70.1	307
Internalizers	48.6	29.9	262
N	492	77	569

$$\chi^2(1) = 9.38, p = .002, \phi = .13$$

Note.—The proportion of Externalizers was greater in AFDC families.

F. Aid for Women, Infants, and Children (WIC)

	No	Yes	N
Externalizers	53.2	69.2	307
Internalizers	46.8	30.8	262
N	543	26	569

$$\chi^2(1) = 2.56, p = .110, \phi = .07$$

Note.—No significant relation between WIC and E-I scores.

G. Food Stamps

	No	Yes	N
Externalizing	51.0	70.5	308
Internalizing	49.0	29.6	262
N	482	88	570

$$\chi^2(1) = 11.30, p < .001, \phi = .14$$

Note.—The proportion of Externalizers was greater in food stamp families.

H. Unemployment Benefits

	No	Yes	N
Externalizers	53.8	61.5	307
Internalizers	46.2	38.5	262
N	556	13	569

$$\chi^2(1) = .31, p = .579, \phi = .02$$

Note.—No significant relation between unemployment benefits and E-I scores.

I. Other Government Assistance

	No	Yes	N
Externalizers	51.9	71.7	307
Internalizers	48.1	28.3	262
N	509	60	569

$$\chi^2(1) = 8.47, p = .004, \phi = .12$$

Note.—The proportion of Externalizers was greater in families receiving other government assistance.

TABLE 12 (*Continued*)

J. Any Form of Government Assistance

	No	Yes	N
Externalizers	49.0	67.5	308
Internalizers	51.0	32.5	262
N	416	154	570

$$\chi^2(1) = 15.48, p < .001, \phi = .17$$

NOTE.—The proportion of Externalizers was greater in families receiving any assistance.

K. Number of Household and Family Members Receiving Mental Health Services (Besides Subject)

	0	1	> 1	N
Externalizers	10.1	17.4	20.9	308
Intermediate	81.1	69.9	57.1	2,157
Internalizers	8.7	12.7	22.0	262
N	2,337	299	91	2,727

$$\chi^2(4) = 49.32, p < .001, \phi = .13$$

NOTE.—The more members receiving mental health services, the greater the proportion of both Externalizers and Internalizers.

[a] Subjects were classified as Externalizers or Internalizers relative to the entire survey sample of 2,600 nonreferred, 46 extra subjects, and 88 referred subjects. N was reduced by missing or unclassifiable data for some items. Chi square analyses were based on actual cell frequencies, but, to aid the reader, the cell frequencies are displayed in terms of the percentage of subjects in each column who were classified by each level of the variable.

the scores were computed within two-year age intervals only for the entire survey sample of 2,734—these are not the same scores obtained by standardizing within the matched referred and nonreferred samples of 2,600 that were reported earlier.)

Children were classified as "Externalizers" if their E-I scores were above the 90th percentile, that is, their Externalizing scores exceeded their Internalizing scores by more than was found for the remaining 90% of the sample. They were classified as "Internalizers" if their E-I scores were at or below the 10th percentile, that is, their Internalizing scores exceeded their Externalizing scores by more than was found for the remaining 90% of the sample. The remaining 80% of the children were classified as an intermediate group.

We computed chi squares for relations between the dichotomous Externalizing-Internalizing classification and the family variables, as shown in Table 12. As in Table 11, the data are displayed as percentages of each column to aid the reader in seeing relations between each family characteristic and the E-I classification. The chi squares revealed significantly elevated proportions of Externalizers in households where parents were unmarried, separated, or divorced and in those receiving each of the kinds of public assistance other than WIC and unemployment benefits. There was also a borderline significant tendency (p = .075) for households with unrelated adults to have a higher proportion of Externalizing than Internalizing children.

As indicated in Table 12, the proportions of both Externalizers and Internalizers were significantly elevated where household or family members other than the child had received mental health services. A t test also showed higher Externalizing z scores in the 60 cases where depressive diagnoses were reported than in demographically matched cases where no mental health services were reported (t = 2.23, p = .030). Not enough other diagnoses could be classified into particular categories for analysis.

Most of the family variables associated with high total problem scores (as shown in Table 11) were associated more strongly with Externalizing patterns than Internalizing patterns. By contrast, however, receipt of mental health services by family members was associated with elevated rates of Internalizing as well as Externalizing patterns. It thus appears that family mental health history is a risk factor not only for behavioral/emotional problems in general but for distinctive patterns of problems that represent both extremes on the Internalizing-Externalizing continuum.

VIII. COMPARISONS WITH OTHER STUDIES

Many kinds of research are needed to advance our knowledge of child psychopathology. Among the most fundamental are efforts to improve the empirical basis for our concepts of disorders. This requires identification of criterial attributes that can be used to define disorders both conceptually and operationally. The present study was designed to contribute to such efforts by testing a method and using it to obtain data nationwide as a basis for advancing concepts and procedures for defining disorders.

Previous studies using the CBCL have tested the ability of specific problem and competence items to discriminate between referred and nonreferred children within a single region of a country (Achenbach & Edelbrock, 1981; Montenegro, 1983; Verhulst, Akkerhuis, & Althaus, 1985). In earlier chapters, we compared the psychometric properties of the ACQ with the properties of the CBCL. Other studies have assessed small sets of problem items in national samples (e.g., Fogelman, 1976; National Center for Health Statistics, 1982; Zill & Peterson, 1982) or have done more extensive assessments of local or regional samples (e.g., Bird, Gould, Yager, Staghezza, & Canino, 1989; Offord et al., 1987; Rutter, Tizard, & Whitmore, 1970). No previous studies, however, were designed to compare such an extensive set of problems and competencies in clinical versus nonclinical samples across such major regional, ethnic, environmental, and socioeconomic variations as are found throughout the continental United States.

Traditional epidemiological studies aim to determine the prevalence and distribution of disorders and their correlates in particular populations. To achieve such aims, it is necessary to have clear taxonomic constructs for the target disorders and methodologically sound assessment procedures for operationally defining the constructs. Our study was not a traditional epidemiological study because it was not designed to tabulate prevalence rates for preconceived disorders. Instead, it was designed to test the discriminative power and correlates of specific items and scales for their potential contribution to empirically based taxonomic constructs and assessment procedures for childhood disorders. Testing items and scales in this way constitutes one facet of a program of research that also entails longitudinal research to test the predictive power of the items and scales.

Because this study was not designed to tabulate prevalence rates for preconceived disorders, it cannot be directly compared with the tabulations reported in traditional epidemiological studies. However, findings with respect to specific items, scale scores, and their correlates can be compared with analogous data from other studies, as is done in the following sections.

EFFECTS ASSOCIATED WITH SUBJECT CHARACTERISTICS

Sex differences.—When sex differences in overall problem scores or prevalence rates of disorders have been found in other studies of general population samples, they have typically indicated more problems for boys than girls (Anderson, Williams, McGee, & Silva, 1987; Bird et al., 1989; Offord et al., 1987; Rutter et al., 1970; Verhulst et al., 1985; see also Costello, 1989). However, these differences have tended to be small, and not all studies have found statistically significant sex differences in overall problem rates (e.g., Achenbach & Edelbrock, 1981; Velez, Johnson, & Cohen, 1989).

In our analyses of 2,600 nonreferred children, there was no significant sex difference in total problem scores, although boys scored significantly higher than girls on a significantly greater proportion of specific problem items. Boys also scored higher than girls on more problems in the analyses of the 5,200 matched referred and nonreferred subjects, where the sex difference in total problem scores did reach significance, although it accounted for less than 1% of the variance.

Comparisons of the types of problems on which boys or girls scored higher showed that boys tended to score higher on Externalizing problems and syndromes whereas girls tended to score higher on Internalizing problems and syndromes. In our analyses of the 2,600 nonreferred subjects as well as the 5,200 matched subjects, the total Externalizing score and the E-I score were higher for boys, while the Internalizing score was higher for girls. Other studies have also reported higher rates of Externalizing problems for boys and Internalizing problems for girls (Anderson et al., 1987; Costello et al., 1988; Offord et al., 1987; Rutter et al., 1970; Velez et al., 1989). However, these studies did not provide a basis for directly comparing the relative predominance of Externalizing versus Internalizing problems in normative and clinical samples.

Our comparisons of matched referred and nonreferred samples revealed that the prevailing sex differences in E-I scores were much more pronounced among children deviant enough to be referred for mental health services than among demographically matched nonreferred children, as illustrated in Figure 4. This finding indicates that the sex difference in the predominance of Externalizing versus Internalizing problems is small among relatively normal children but that, among troubled children, there is a considerably greater predominance of Externalizing problems among boys and Internalizing problems among adolescent girls. Whatever factors lead to the sex differences in these problems among normal children thus appear to be exacerbated among troubled children. This does not mean, however, that troubled boys manifest only Externalizing syndromes and troubled girls only Internalizing syndromes. Our factor analyses of large clinical samples indicate that both types of syndromes occur to some degree in both sexes (Achenbach et al., 1989).

Age differences.—Age differences in problems have not been analyzed as extensively as sex differences because fewer studies have spanned wide enough age ranges to justify such analyses. Among studies that used a uniform assessment procedure over ages 4–16, Bird et al. (1989) did not find significant age differences in the total number of DSM-III disorders either with or without the additional criterion of overall impairment, as judged from the Children's Global Assessment Scale (CGAS). For some disorders, Offord, Boyle, and Racine (1989) found complex interactions between age groups 4–11 versus 12–16 and sex of the child, although the findings also depended on whether the informant was the parent, teacher, or child.

In studies that used methodology and age spans similar to those of the present study, a gradual decline in problem scores was found from age 4 to age 16 in nonreferred general population samples (Achenbach & Edelbrock, 1981; Achenbach, Hensley, Phares, & Grayson, 1990; Verhulst et al., 1985). In addition, the CBCL total problem score obtained in the Bird et al. (1989) Puerto Rican study showed a tendency to decline with age that did not differ significantly from that for a demographically matched subset of the Achenbach and Edelbrock (1981) nonreferred sample (see Achenbach, Bird, et al., 1990).

In the present study, age effects took different forms on different items and scales. In the nonreferred sample, there was a significant tendency for total problem scores to decline with age, but there was an opposite tendency in the referred sample, resulting in a significant interaction of clinical status with age in the ANCOVA of 5,200 referred and nonreferred subjects.

The ANCOVA of E-I scores showed a significant linear trend for Externalizing scores to decline with age relative to Internalizing scores. However, like the sex differences in E-I scores, the age differences were significantly more pronounced in the referred than the nonreferred sample, as illustrated in Figure 4.

Because it may be only in adolescence that certain types of Externalizing problems, such as truancy, emerge sufficiently to reach the DSM criteria specified for conduct disorders, an increased rate of DSM-III diagnoses of conduct disorders might be taken to imply an actual increase with age in conduct type problems (e.g., Offord et al., 1989). Although scores on our Delinquent syndrome did increase significantly with age, scores on the Aggressive syndrome decreased significantly with age. Furthermore, when we analyzed broad aggregations of Externalizing versus Internalizing problems in relation to each other, it was evident that the overall E-I mix moved increasingly toward the Internalizing pole across ages 4–16. Longitudinal data are needed to test the developmental hypothesis, but our cross-sectional data indicate a decreasing dominance of Externalizing problems and an increasing dominance of Internalizing problems, especially in children deviant enough to be referred for mental health services.

Ethnic differences.—Few other studies have compared problem rates among ethnic groups where other important variables such as SES, sex, age, and region could be controlled. In samples that included a few blacks from Pittsburgh, Pennsylvania, and two upstate New York counties, Costello (1989) and Velez et al. (1989) reported somewhat higher rates of Externalizing disorders for blacks than whites diagnosed according to DSM-III criteria.

In much larger samples of both blacks and whites, Achenbach and Edelbrock found no significant ethnic differences in total problem scores when SES, sex, age, and referral status were controlled. In analyses of 118 CBCL problem items, eight items showed higher scores for whites, while six showed higher scores for blacks. None of the ethnic effects accounted for more than 1% of the variance, and there was no consistent tendency for either ethnic group to score higher than the other on Internalizing or Externalizing problems.

In the present study, about 75% of the subjects were non-Hispanic white, 16% were black, and the others were of mixed or other ethnicity, as summarized in Table 3. The largest number of the latter group were Hispanic, but there were not enough Hispanics distributed across the SES, sex, age, and geographic variables to allow rigorous comparisons with other ethnic groups while controlling for these variables. We therefore compared non-Hispanic whites with all other groups and blacks with all other groups.

In the ANCOVAs of 5,200 referred and nonreferred subjects, there were significant differences between non-Hispanic white and other ethnic groups on 40 ACQ problem items, three syndromes, Externalizing, and total problem score. Most of the differences involved slightly higher scores for non-Hispanic whites than other ethnic groups, but all differences accounted for less than 1% of the variance. The comparisons of black versus other ethnic groups yielded significant differences on only 19 problem items, with blacks scoring higher on only 6 and all differences accounting for less than 1% of the variance. Very similar findings were obtained when the nonreferred sample of 2,600 was analyzed separately. In the ANCOVA of E-I scores, the covariate for black versus other ethnic groups indicated a slight tendency for black parents to report proportionally more Externalizing than Internalizing problems. However, this effect accounted for only .1% of the variance, and it does not indicate more Externalizing problems for blacks than other ethnic groups because the only ethnic effect on the magnitude of Externalizing scores per se indicated slightly higher scores among non-Hispanic whites than other ethnic groups. When other demographic variables were controlled in our national sample, ethnic differences were thus minuscule with respect to the parent-reported problems assessed in this study.

EFFECTS ASSOCIATED WITH FAMILY CHARACTERISTICS

Socioeconomic differences.—Most studies of SES differences have reported more problems and diagnosed disorders among lower-SES than higher-SES children (e.g., Achenbach & Edelbrock, 1981; Bird et al., 1989; Offord et al., 1989; Velez et al., 1989; Verhulst et al., 1985). We likewise found that most SES effects on problem items and scale scores indicated more problems for lower-SES children. Like the sex and age differences, the SES differences were more pronounced in analyses that included referred children than in analyses of nonreferred children alone. This was indicated by the finding of 127 significant SES effects in the ANCOVAs that included referred children, compared to 41 significant effects in the parallel ANCOVAs of nonreferred children alone. However, even in the analyses that included referred children, none of the effects accounted for more than 1% of the variance. The tendency for lower-SES children to obtain higher total problem scores accounted for only .3% of the variance. Thus, although SES was significantly associated with problem scores, it represented a very small effect. It manifested an even smaller though significant association with E-I scores (.1% of variance), where lower-SES children tended to have higher Externalizing than Internalizing scores.

Family risk variables.—Several family variables assessed by our interviewers were found to be significantly associated with high ACQ problem scores. These included (*a*) parents who were unmarried, separated, or divorced rather than married or widowed; (*b*) relatively few related adults in the child's household; (*c*) relatively many unrelated adults in the child's household; (*d*) receipt of public assistance; and (*e*) receipt of mental health services by family or household members.

Other studies have also reported higher rates of problems in children whose families were disrupted, were financially disadvantaged, or had psychiatric histories (e.g., Anderson et al., 1987; Bird et al., 1989; Costello, 1989; Offord et al., 1989; Velez et al., 1989). However, our finding that the proportion of children having high problem scores decreased steadily with increases in the number of related adults in the household suggests a protective role for adult family members even beyond the protective value of living with both parents. Yet the finding that the proportion of high problem scores increased with increases in the number of unrelated adults suggests that it is not adults per se but those having family attachments who play a protective role with respect to children's problems.

Our analyses of E-I scores showed that parental marital status and public assistance were associated not only with elevated problem scores in general but also with a relative dominance of Externalizing over Internalizing problems. By contrast, receipt of mental health services by family or household members was associated with elevated rates of both a dominance of Externalizing problems and a dominance of Internalizing problems. In other words, most of the risk factors were associated with Externalizing patterns, whereas mental health services were associated with both the Externalizing and the Internalizing extremes but lower rates of intermediate mixtures of these types of problems.

EFFECTS ASSOCIATED WITH URBANIZATION

It is often assumed that cities are bad for children. Some American cities have become notorious for inner-city poverty, poor school achievement, and high crime rates. Efforts to assess the mental health of urban children have generally contrasted such children with those living in rural environments (e.g., Kastrup, 1977; Lavik, 1977; Offord et al., 1987; Rutter, Cox, Tupling, Berger, & Yule, 1975).

In a review of his own classic Isle of Wight and Inner London Borough studies, as well as research by others, Rutter (1981) concluded that problem prevalence rates were indeed higher for urban children. He viewed the higher prevalence rates as by-products of the higher rates of family disruption in inner cities than in rural areas. Later research in Ontario has supported Rutter's findings of higher prevalence rates for disorders in urban than rural areas (Offord et al., 1987).

The findings of higher problem rates in urban than rural areas agrees with common impressions. There has, however, evidently been little effort to perform finer-grained analyses of gradations of urbanization when factors such as SES and ethnicity were controlled. The selection of our survey sample from 100 PSUs distributed across the 48 contiguous states provided an opportunity to compare problem rates for large cities with those for smaller urban areas as well as rural areas while controlling for other demographic variables.

As a first pass, we compared children from the most urban versus the most rural PSUs. If there were a linear effect of urbanization per se, it should be evident in this comparison between the PSUs differing most in urbanization. A 2 (urban vs. rural) × 2 (sex) × 7 (age group) ANCOVA was performed on each of the eight syndromes, Externalizing, Internalizing, E-I, total problems, three competence scales, and total competence score (for ages 6 and older) for the 140 nonreferred children who came from PSUs in areas of 1,000,000 or more population and the 318 nonreferred children who came from unincorporated rural PSUs. Covariates were SES, non-Hispanic white versus other ethnic groups, and black versus other ethnic groups. The only significant main effect of urbanization was the higher mean score on the Delinquent syndrome for urban than rural children ($F = 9.50$, $p < .01$, accounting for 2% of the variance). This is no more than would be expected by chance in the 16 analyses of urbanization main effects. Of the 48 analyses of interactions with urbanization, only one was significant at $p < .05$, which is less than expected by chance.

A finer-grained comparison was made by forming one-to-one matches between the 140 urban subjects and 140 rural subjects matched to the urban subjects for sex and age and as closely as possible for ethnicity. To obtain enough subjects for close matching of all 140 urban children to rural children on all demographic variables, we included in our pool of candidates all 672 children living in PSUs classified as unurbanized, even though some of these had populations greater than 10,000. In a 2 × 2 × 7 ANCOVA with SES and ethnicity as covariates, there was virtually no difference in total problem scores ($M = 72.3$ for urban vs. 71.6 for rural, $F = 0.0$). Nor were there significant differences between the matched urban and rural children in syndrome scales, Externalizing, Internalizing, E-I, competence scales, or total competence scores. The nearest approximation to a main effect of urbanization was again a higher mean score on the Delinquent syndrome for urban than rural children. However, this difference now reached only $p = .051$ and was less than the three differences expected to reach $p = .05$ by chance in 16 comparisons, using a .05 protection level (Sakoda et al., 1954). The single significant interaction that reached $p = .05$ was also less than expected by chance.

The accessibility of mental health services and the thresholds for referral may differ between urban and rural environments. We therefore compared the most urban PSUs (areas with 1,000,000 or more population) and most rural PSUs with respect to the proportion of the initial survey sample who had received mental health services in the preceding 12 months. (By "initial sample," we mean the sample of 2,600 on whom data were initially obtained before the addition of nonreferred children to substitute for those who were found to have been referred during the previous 12 months.) The proportions of urban versus rural referred children did not differ significantly (2/140 urban = 1.43% vs. 3/317 rural = .95%, $p = .64$ by

Fisher's exact test). Thus, differential referral rates could not explain the lack of significant differences between the total problem scores of urban versus rural children.

Why did we find no significant urban-rural differences between referral rates or competence scores and only a small difference of dubious statistical significance on a single measure of problems? Examination of the comparisons presented by Offord et al. (1987) and Rutter (1981) showed that variables other than degree of urbanization were associated with their urban versus rural comparisons. As Rutter pointed out, differences in the prevalence of family disruption appeared to contribute to the differences in problem prevalence rates between the Isle of Wight and inner-city London. Offord et al., on the other hand, compared all their sampling sites in Ontario that had populations of 25,000 or fewer with those having populations greater than 25,000. Despite the high statistical power afforded by 1,648 urban versus 1,031 rural children, Offord et al. found statistically significant differences only for hyperactivity (7% of urban vs. 4.6% of rural children) and for the presence of any one or more disorders (19.6% of urban vs. 14.9% of rural children). No significant urban-rural differences were found for the other disorders that were analyzed, that is, conduct, emotional, or somatization disorders. Nor did Offord et al. find significant differences between utilization rates for mental health and social services (including courts, Children's Aid, and Family Service) during the preceding 6 months (6.2% of urban vs. 7.0% of rural children).

To explore urbanization effects further, we compared referral rates and total problem scores for children divided according to the following four categories of urbanization: (1) PSUs of 1,000,000 or more population; (2) PSUs of 250,000–999,999 population; (3) PSUs of 10,000–249,999 population; and (4) PSUs ranging from unincorporated rural areas to unurbanized areas of 9,999 population.

A 2 × 4 chi square for the proportion of referred children found in the initial sample of 2,600 showed significant differences among the four categories of urbanization, $\chi^2(3) = 13.65, p = .003$. The referral rates were 1.43% for both category 1 and category 4 but were 5.59% for category 2 and 3.82% for category 3. The odds ratio of 2.95 (95% confidence interval = 1.52–5.74) showed that the referral rate was significantly higher in the two intermediate categories combined than in the most urban and most rural categories combined. The odds ratio of 4.09 (95% confidence interval = 1.85–9.03) between category 2 and the most urban and most rural categories combined showed a still larger difference, but the difference between categories 2 and 3 was not significant.

We then removed the referred subjects and restored their nonreferred replacement subjects to reconstitute the nonreferred sample of 2,600. In the sample of 2,600 nonreferred children, the total problem, total competence, three competence scales, eight syndrome scales, Externalizing, Internalizing, and E-I scores were subjected to 4 (urbanization level) × 2 (sex) × 7 (age group) × 4 (region) ANCOVAs, with SES, non-Hispanic white, and black ethnicity as covariates. Three of the 16 ANCOVAs showed main effects of urbanization that were significant at $p < .01$, each accounting for 1% of the variance. There were no significant interactions with urbanization. Contrasts testing the three main effects indicated significantly higher scores on the Withdrawn, Delinquent, and Internalizing scales for children from both the intermediate urbanization levels than for children from the most rural areas. Children from the most urban level also had significantly higher scores than children from the most rural area on the Delinquent syndrome. Although this again suggested a small tendency for the most urban children to have higher rates of delinquent behavior than the most rural children, it was the children in areas of intermediate urbanization who differed most from the most rural children. This is borne out in the trends for total problem scores, which were higher for the intermediate urbanization categories ($M = 75.8$ for category 2 and 74.2 for category 3) than for category 1 ($M = 71.5$) or category 4 ($M = 69.7$). This suggests that the significantly higher referral rates in the areas of intermediate urbanization were not artifacts of better access to services or lower thresholds for referral, given a particular level of problems. Instead, even after referred children were removed from the sample, the problem scores for the nonreferred children tended to be higher in the two intermediate areas than in the most urban or most rural areas.

Previous conclusions that problem rates are higher in urban than rural areas may have reflected the tendency to combine areas of intermediate urbanization with large urban areas for comparison with rural areas as well as a possible lack of control for demographic differences. Insofar as urbanization is associated with problem and referral rates at all, the present evidence suggests very small and nonlinear effects, at least in the United States, when demographic differences are controlled.

Urbanization was not significantly related to competence scale scores in any analyses paralleling those just described for problem scores. This indicates that large urban, small urban, and rural areas did not differentially affect children's opportunities to obtain favorable scores on our competence scales, despite differences in the types of activities that may be available.

IX. SUMMARY AND CONCLUSIONS

We compared parent-reported problems and competencies in 2,600 children assessed at 18 mental health services and 2,600 nonreferred children assessed in a home interview survey at 100 sites representative of the 48 contiguous states. The target samples were 100 referred and 100 nonreferred children of each sex at ages 4–16. However, inaccuracies in the initial statements of birth dates and shortfalls in some strata produced small deviations from the target N of 100 in each cell, necessitating inclusion of one 3-year-old and two 17-year-olds in the nonreferred sample and three 3-year-olds and five 17-year-olds in the referred sample.

Parents responded to the ACQ Behavior Checklist, which comprises 23 competence items and 216 problem items. It is also scored in terms of three competence scales, a total competence score, eight syndromes, Internalizing, Externalizing, and a total problem score. In the referred sample, parents completed the ACQ as part of the intake procedure where their children were being evaluated for mental health services. In the home interview survey, an interviewer handed the respondent a copy of the ACQ, read the items aloud from a second copy, and entered the respondent's answers on the interviewer's copy. The overall completion rate was 92.1% for interviews with parents of identified eligible children.

PSYCHOMETRIC FINDINGS

Reliability.—Over a mean interval of 8.2 days, the r for test-retest reliability was .91 for total competence scores and .88 for total problem scores, although there was also a significant decline in reported problems over this period. Test-retest intraclass correlations were 1.00 across the mean scores for individual competence items and .89 across the problem items. The interparent r was .72 for both the total competence score and the total problem score, although mothers reported significantly more problems than fathers. The interparent intraclass correlations were .96 across mean scores for individual competence items and .93 across problem items. For demographically matched subjects where only the mother or the father served as the informant, there were no significant differences between scores obtained from mothers and fathers in either the referred or the nonreferred samples. This indicates that our overall findings were not affected by which parent completed the ACQ.

Validity.—The concurrent validity of the ACQ total problem score was supported by r's of .88 with the Achenbach CBCL, .78 with the Quay-Peterson RBPC, and .68 with the Conners PQ. Discriminant validity was supported by significantly higher scores on 209 of the 216 problem items in referred than in demographically matched nonreferred children as well as on all eight syndromes, Externalizing, Internalizing, and total problem score and by significantly lower scores on 20 of the 23 competence items, three competence scales, and total competence score. In addition, subjects in the survey sample who were found to have received mental health services in the preceding 12 months obtained significantly higher problem scores and lower competence scores than demographically matched survey children who had not received mental health services during the preceding 12 months. The survey versus clinical context for data collection was thus unlikely to account for the differences found between the referred and the nonreferred samples.

Psychometric comparisons with the CBCL.—The mean scores obtained on the ACQ problem items by our nonreferred subjects and scores obtained by nonreferred subjects on 115 CBCL counterpart items in five other samples showed correlations ranging from .72 for a Thai sample to .92 for the 1976 Washington, DC, area sample. Beside the Washington, DC, sample, the only other English-language CBCL nonreferred sample—from Sydney, Australia—correlated .89 with the ACQ item scores. Mean item scores in the ACQ clinical sample correlated .95 with mean scores in the CBCL clinical sample. There was thus considerable similarity in the rank ordering of problem scores across samples, despite differences in language, culture, and time when the data were collected.

Differences between referred and nonreferred samples showed larger effects on the item and scale scores of the CBCL than on the ACQ. Several kinds of evidence indicated that the ACQ's four-step response scale reduced differences between referred and nonreferred samples by leading parents of nonreferred children to avoid the bottom step on the scale and parents of referred children to avoid the top step. The four-step scale may also be more vulnerable to respondent variables, causing larger differences between test-retest and mother-father ACQ ratings than were found on the CBCL.

DEMOGRAPHIC FINDINGS

Sex differences.—In ANCOVAs of 2,600 referred versus 2,600 nonreferred subjects, boys scored significantly higher than girls on 84 problem items, three syndromes, Externalizing, and the total problem score. Girls scored significantly higher on 46 problem items, two syndromes, and Internalizing. Boys obtained significantly higher scores on three competence items, while girls obtained higher scores on 12 competence items, the School scale, and the total competence score. Only one sex difference was large enough to qualify as a medium effect according to Cohen's (1988) criteria. Reflecting higher scores for boys, this sex difference accounted for 10% of the variance in item 7. *Admires tough guys,* where the masculine connotation of "guys" may have contributed to the difference. Most other sex differences accounted for less than 1% of variance. The tendency for more problems to be reported for boys is consistent with the findings of other studies that have reported sex differences.

Age differences.—Age differences were larger and more numerous than sex differences, being found on 172 problem items, seven syndromes, Internalizing, 22 competence items, the three competence scales, and total competence. Some effects of age reflected higher scores for younger children, some higher scores for older children, and some nonlinear age patterns. Age differences reached Cohen's criteria for medium effects on seven problem items and one competence item. As found in the few directly comparable studies, problem scores tended to decline with age for nonreferred children. However, an opposite tendency for referred children produced a significant interaction between clinical status and age.

Regional differences.—In the ANCOVAs of 2,600 referred versus 2,600 nonreferred subjects, regional differences were smaller and less numerous than age or sex differences. Only one regional difference accounted for as much as 1% of the variance in a problem score, and two accounted for as much as 2% of the variance in competence scores. The directions of the regional effects varied widely.

SES differences.—Based on a comparison of nine SES indices involving parental occupation, education, and household income, we chose Hollingshead (1975) scores for the occupation of the higher-status parent as our SES index. Most SES differences reflected higher problem and lower competence scores for lower-SES than higher-SES children. Although significant SES differences were found on 116 problem items, seven syndromes, Internalizing, Externalizing, and the total problem score, none of these accounted for more than 1% of the variance. Of the significant SES differences found on 21 competence items, three competence scales, and total competence score, the largest accounted for 5% of the variance in item *IVA*.

Number of organizations and in the total competence score. Both these effects reflected lower scores for lower-SES than higher-SES children. Our findings of somewhat higher problem and lower competence scores among lower-SES children are consistent with other studies that have assessed these relations.

Ethnic differences.—Ethnic differences had fewer associations with problem and competence scores than did the other demographic variables. The covariate of non-Hispanic white versus other ethnic groups showed significant associations with 40 problem items, three syndromes, Externalizing, total problem score, and eight competence scores. Most of the differences reflected higher problem and competence scores for non-Hispanic whites. However, all the effects were tiny, with only one of the effects on a problem score accounting for as much as .8% of variance and no effects on competence scores accounting for as much as .5% of variance. The covariate of black versus other ethnic groups showed significant associations with only 19 problem items and two competence items, the latter being no more than expected by chance. Our 1981 CBCL study also showed minimal differences between reports by black and white parents. None of the effects accounted for as much as 1% of the variance. Other studies have not tested ethnic differences while controlling for sex, age, SES, region, and referral status.

Nonreferred children.—To obtain a picture of demographic effects in our nationally representative sample of nonreferred children taken alone, we also performed separate ANCOVAs of all item and scale scores obtained by the 2,600 nonreferred children. Even though statistical power remained asymptotically high in this sample of 2,600, there were considerably fewer significant associations of problem scores with sex, age, region, and SES than in the ANCOVAs that included referred children. The decrease in significant associations probably reflected the smaller variance in problem scores in relation to the demographic variables among nonreferred children than when referred children were included. That is, the sex, age, regional, and SES differences in problems were more pronounced when referred children were included than among their nonreferred counterparts taken alone. The small number of ethnic effects remained about the same in the nonreferred sample as when combined with the referred sample.

In the analyses of competence scores among the 2,600 nonreferred subjects, there were also somewhat fewer significant associations with sex, age, region, and SES but about the same number of associations with ethnicity. However, the SES effects on academic performance, the School scale, and total problem scores were *larger* in the nonreferred sample than when combined with the referred sample. This indicated that, among troubled children, scores in these areas were more uniformly low regardless of SES.

Externalizing versus Internalizing.—To assess the degree to which subjects were reported to have Externalizing versus Internalizing problems, we computed an Externalizing-Internalizing (E-I) score consisting of a z score for Externalizing minus a z score for Internalizing. Across the 5,200 referred and nonreferred subjects, the E-I scores showed significant interactions of clinical status with sex and age. As illustrated in Figure 4, boys had a larger proportion of Externalizing problems than girls, but this sex difference was greater among referred than nonreferred subjects. Furthermore, there was a steeper decline in the proportion of Externalizing problems with age for referred than for nonreferred subjects of both sexes.

DISCRIMINATION BETWEEN THE NORMAL AND THE CLINICAL RANGE

We compared several procedures for using the ACQ to discriminate between children who are in the normal versus clinical range of functioning, using our demographically matched nonreferred and referred samples as criterion groups. The most efficient cut points on the total problem scores ranged from the 80th to the 85th percentile for each sex analyzed separately at ages 4–5, 6–11, and 12–16. These cut points produced a mean misclassification rate of 26.7%. A criterion for deviance defined as total problem scores above the 80th percentile and competence scores at or below the 20th percentile produced a mean misclassification rate of 28.6%. When children who were deviant on one score but not the other were classified as "mixed," the mean misclassification rate dropped to 14.3%, with 33.4% in the mixed category. Specificity was 94.8%, whereas sensitivity was 76.6%.

Discriminant analyses using the total problem and competence scores as predictors produced a mean cross-validated misclassification rate of 26.2%, with specificity of 84.8% and sensitivity of 62.8%. Stepwise discriminant analyses selecting all competence and syndrome scales that significantly ($p < .05$) contributed to discrimination produced a mean cross-validated misclassification rate of 20.5% with specificity of 85.2% and sensitivity of 73.7%. Similar discriminant analyses using competence and problem items as predictors produced a mean cross-validated misclassification rate of 13.3% with specificity of 92.1% and sensitivity of 80.4%.

Misclassifications could be substantially reduced by allowing a mixed or borderline category of children who were not clearly in either the normal or the clinical range. For the sake of comparisons between cut points on the total problem scores alone and the discriminant analyses, we defined the borderline group as those subjects who scored between the 81st and the 90th percentiles on the total problem score. Allowing these subjects to remain borderline (not forced into normal vs. clinical categories) improved the misclassification rate to 22.8% using the 90th percentile cut point on the total problem score and 23.9% using the total problem and competence scores in discriminant analyses, although it did not improve on the use of the individual problem and competence items in discriminant analyses. Because a borderline category can be useful for identifying cases that require further evaluation or deferral of decisions, it provides a more realistic way of representing decision procedures than a model that forces all individuals into a "sick" versus "well" dichotomy.

FAMILIAL CORRELATES OF PROBLEMS

Besides responding to the ACQ, parents in the home interview survey were asked questions about family constellations, marital status, child-care arrangements, public assistance, and mental health services (App. D). These were analyzed in relation to problem scores and E-I scores in the entire survey sample of 2,734, including children who had been excluded from the nonreferred sample of 2,600 because they had received mental health services during the preceding year or because they duplicated subjects in cells that were already filled.

The following were significantly associated with high ACQ problem scores: fewer related adults in the household; more unrelated adults in the household; parents who were separated, divorced, or never married to each other; receipt of public assistance; and receipt of mental health services by household or family members. E-I scores indicating a predominance of Externalizing problems were significantly associated with parents who were separated, divorced, or never married to each other and receipt of public assistance. Receipt of mental health services was associated with elevated rates of both extremes of E-I scores, that is, with children who showed primarily Externalizing patterns and children who showed primarily Internalizing patterns.

Other studies have reported elevated problem rates in children whose families were disrupted, were financially disadvantaged, or had psychiatric histories. However, the opposite relations between children's problems and the number of related versus unrelated adults and the association of familial mental health services with both Externalizing and Internalizing patterns have evidently not been reported previously.

URBANIZATION

Other studies have reported higher problem rates among urban than rural children. They have not, however, compared varying degrees of urbanization while controlling for sex, age, referral status, SES, region, and ethnicity. We found little difference between either the referral rates or the problem scores for children living in the most urban versus the most rural areas. Areas of intermediate urbanization, however, showed significantly higher referral rates, plus a tendency toward higher problem scores among nonreferred children, than did the most urban and the most rural areas. Competence scores were not significantly associated with urbanization.

GENERAL CONCLUSIONS

We believe that the present study provides data on a more extensive range of problems and competencies assessed in a more representative national sample over a wider age range than any previously published study. It demonstrates the feasibility of economically obtaining data on nationally representative samples with which to test important demographic variables, to establish baselines against which secular and developmental changes can be assessed, and to provide standards of comparison for findings in local or less representative samples.

Standardized rating forms such as the ACQ are far less costly than the main alternatives for collecting similar data, such as the Diagnostic Interview Schedule for Children (DISC; Shaffer, Fisher, Piacentini, Schwab-Stone, & Wicks, 1989). Whereas interviews require intensively trained interviewers and hours to administer and score, rating forms like the ACQ can be self-administered. In our study, interviewers were used to ensure that the appropriate informants were reached, that respondent reading skills were not a factor, and that other data were obtained. However, the interviewers did not require extensive training, the administration time was 20–35 min (in contrast to 1–2 hours for interviews like the DISC), and responses were precoded on a single four-page form for easy data entry. Furthermore, rating forms like the ACQ can be economically used in a great variety of situations, such as surveys, clinical settings, schools, and by mail, and they can be easily translated for use in other languages. The versatility, economy, and robustness of this approach has been demonstrated by the use of the CBCL and its related forms in over 700 published studies, with translations into 33 languages (Achenbach & Brown, 1991). Because it has only about half as many items, the CBCL also takes less time than the ACQ to administer.

The findings revealed numerous and large differences between the problem scores of demographically matched referred and nonreferred children. Important age and sex variations were also found. Geographic and ethnic differences were minimal. Urbanization effects on problem scores were minimal, but clinical referral rates were highest in areas of intermediate urbanization. SES differences were more pervasive but accounted for a very small percentage of variance in problem items, though somewhat more variance in competence items. Several family risk factors were significantly associated with problem scores.

The minimal geographic, ethnic, and urbanization effects mean that these variables are not apt to constrain the generalizability of findings with the ACQ. The small SES effects are consistent with other studies in showing somewhat more problems and fewer competencies among lower-SES groups, as reported by teachers and children themselves, as well as by parents (e.g., Achenbach & Edelbrock, 1986, 1987; Verhulst & Akkerhuis, 1986). Although we were able to collect data only from parents in the present study, we have since been able to carry out a 3-year follow-up of the survey sample in which parent, teacher, and self-reports were obtained. The follow-up data will enable us to test the multivariate predictive power of all the variables assessed in the present study, combined with data on intervening stresses and familial changes.

APPENDIX A

ACQ BEHAVIOR CHECKLIST

Please answer all items as well as you can, even if some do not seem to apply to your child. Feel free to write additional comments wherever you wish.

Child's Age _____ Race or ethnic group _____

Today's date: Month _____ Day _____ Year _____   Sex: ☐ Boy ☐ Girl   This form filled out by:

☐ Mother
☐ Father
☐ Other (specify) _____

Parents' type of work: Please state the kind of job parent usually does (**not** name of firm). For example: Homemaker, auto mechanic, high school teacher, army sergeant, even if parent does not live with child.   **Father's** type of work _____   **Mother's** type of work _____

Child's birth: Month _____ Day _____ Year _____

Parents' education:

	Grade 1-9	Grade 10-12	High School Graduate	1-4 Yrs. College	College Graduate	Postgraduate Degree (specify)	Other (specify)
Father	☐	☐	☐	☐	☐	_____	_____
Mother	☐	☐	☐	☐	☐	_____	_____

I. Please list the sports your child most likes to take part in. For example: swimming, baseball, skating, skate boarding, bike riding, fishing, etc.

☐ None

		Compared to other children of the same age, about how much time does he/she spend in each?				Compared to other children of the same age, how well does he/she do each one?			
		Don't Know	Less Than Average	Average	More Than Average	Don't Know	Below Average	Average	Above Average
A.	_____	☐	☐	☐	☐	☐	☐	☐	☐
B.	_____	☐	☐	☐	☐	☐	☐	☐	☐
C.	_____	☐	☐	☐	☐	☐	☐	☐	☐
D.	_____	☐	☐	☐	☐	☐	☐	☐	☐

II. Please list your child's favorite hobbies, activities, and games, other than sports. For example: stamps, dolls, books, piano, crafts, etc. (Do **not** include listening to radio or T.V.)

☐ None

		Compared to other children of the same age, about how much time does he/she spend in each?				Compared to other children of the same age, how well does he/she do each one?			
		Don't Know	Less Than Average	Average	More Than Average	Don't Know	Below Average	Average	Above Average
A.	_____	☐	☐	☐	☐	☐	☐	☐	☐
B.	_____	☐	☐	☐	☐	☐	☐	☐	☐
C.	_____	☐	☐	☐	☐	☐	☐	☐	☐
D.	_____	☐	☐	☐	☐	☐	☐	☐	☐

III. Please list any jobs or chores your child has. For example: paper route, babysitting, making bed, etc.

☐ None

		Compared to other children of the same age, how well does he/she carry them out?			
		Don't Know	Below Average	Average	Above Average
A.	_____	☐	☐	☐	☐
B.	_____	☐	☐	☐	☐
C.	_____	☐	☐	☐	☐
D.	_____	☐	☐	☐	☐

IV. Please list any organizations, clubs, teams, or groups your child belongs to.

☐ None

		Compared to other children of the same age, how active is he/she in each?			
		Don't Know	Less Active	Average	More Active
A.	_____	☐	☐	☐	☐
B.	_____	☐	☐	☐	☐
C.	_____	☐	☐	☐	☐
D.	_____	☐	☐	☐	☐

1-87 Edition

V. **A. About how many close friends does your child have?** ☐ None ☐ 1 ☐ 2 or 3 ☐ 4 or more

B. About how many times a week does your child do things with friends outside of regular school hours? ☐ less than 1 ☐ 1 or 2 ☐ 3 or more

VI. Compared to other children of his/her age, how well does your child:

	Worse	About Average	Better	
A. Get along with his/her brothers & sisters?	☐	☐	☐	☐ Has no brothers or sisters
B. Get along with other children?	☐	☐	☐	
C. Behave with his/her parents?	☐	☐	☐	
D. Work alone?	☐	☐	☐	
E. Play or other leisure activities alone?	☐	☐	☐	

VII. **A. Current school performance—for children aged 6 and older:**

☐ Does not go to school

	Failing	Below Average	Average	Above Average	Far Above Average
1. Reading or English	☐	☐	☐	☐	☐
2. Arithmetic or Math	☐	☐	☐	☐	☐
3. History or Social Studies	☐	☐	☐	☐	☐
4. Science	☐	☐	☐	☐	☐
Other academic subjects—for example: foreign language, spelling, writing 5. _____	☐	☐	☐	☐	☐
6. _____	☐	☐	☐	☐	☐
7. _____	☐	☐	☐	☐	☐

B. Is your child in a special class or special school?

☐ No   ☐ Yes—what kind?

C. Has your child ever repeated a grade?

☐ No   ☐ Yes—grade and reason

D. Has your child had any academic or other problems in school?

☐ No   ☐ Yes—please describe

When did these problems start? _____   Have these problems ended? ☐ No   ☐ Yes—when?

VIII. Please describe the best things about your child _____
_____
_____

IX. What concerns you most about your child? _____
_____
_____

Below is a list of items that describe children. As you read each item, please decide whether it has been true of your child at any time during the **past two months.** Then circle the number that best describes your child:

0 = **Never or not at all true (as far as you know)**　　　　2 = **Quite often or quite a lot**
1 = **Once in awhile or just a little**　　　　3 = **Very often or very much**

1. Absentminded or forgets easily	0 1 2 3	
2. Acts like opposite sex	0 1 2 3	
3. Acts silly or giggles too much	0 1 2 3	
4. Acts spitefully	0 1 2 3	
5. Acts too young for his/her age	0 1 2 3	
6. Admires people who break the law	0 1 2 3	
7. Admires tough guys	0 1 2 3	
8. Afraid of making a mistake	0 1 2 3	
9. Afraid to try new things	0 1 2 3	
10. Always on the go	0 1 2 3	
11. Argues	0 1 2 3	
12. Angry moods	0 1 2 3	
13. Avoids looking others in the eye	0 1 2 3	
14. Bites fingernails	0 1 2 3	
15. Blames others for own mistakes or problems	0 1 2 3	
16. Bossy	0 1 2 3	
17. Bowel movements outside toilet	0 1 2 3	
18. Brags, boasts	0 1 2 3	
19. Bullies or is mean to others	0 1 2 3	
20. Can't concentrate, can't pay attention for long	0 1 2 3	
21. Can't get mind off certain thoughts (give details): _____	0 1 2 3	
22. Can't make up mind or make choices	0 1 2 3	
23. Can't sit still, squirms, or fidgets	0 1 2 3	
24. Can't stand having things out of place	0 1 2 3	
25. Can't stand waiting; wants everything now	0 1 2 3	
26. Cheats	0 1 2 3	
27. Clings to adults or is too dependent	0 1 2 3	
28. Complains too much	0 1 2 3	
29. Complains of aches or pains in arms or legs (without medical cause)	0 1 2 3	
30. Complains of dizziness (without medical cause)	0 1 2 3	
31. Complains of headaches (without medical cause)	0 1 2 3	
32. Complains of loneliness	0 1 2 3	
33. Complains of nausea or feeling sick (without medical cause)	0 1 2 3	
34. Complains of stomach aches or cramps (without medical cause)	0 1 2 3	
35. Confused or seems to be in a fog	0 1 2 3	
36. Constantly asks for help	0 1 2 3	
37. Constipated, doesn't move bowels	0 1 2 3	
38. Cries without good reason	0 1 2 3	
39. Cruel to animals	0 1 2 3	
40. Day-dreams or gets lost in his/her thoughts	0 1 2 3	
41. Defiant	0 1 2 3	
42. Deliberately annoys others	0 1 2 3	
43. Deliberately destroys things belonging to others	0 1 2 3	
44. Deliberately harms self or attempts suicide	0 1 2 3	
45. Deliberately hurts other kids	0 1 2 3	
46. Deliberately tries to vomit	0 1 2 3	
47. Demands attention	0 1 2 3	
48. Destroys his/her own things	0 1 2 3	
49. Diarrhea or loose bowels (without medical cause)	0 1 2 3	
50. Disobedient at home	0 1 2 3	
51. Disobedient at school	0 1 2 3	
52. Does things slowly and incorrectly	0 1 2 3	
53. Doesn't answer when people talk to him/her	0 1 2 3	
54. Doesn't get along with other kids	0 1 2 3	
55. Doesn't seem to feel guilty after misbehaving	0 1 2 3	
56. Doesn't want to go out of home	0 1 2 3	
57. Dresses like or plays at being opposite sex	0 1 2 3	
58. Drowsy, sleepy	0 1 2 3	
59. Easily distracted	0 1 2 3	
60. Easily flustered around other people	0 1 2 3	
61. Easily jealous	0 1 2 3	
62. Eats or drinks things that are not food (give details): _____	0 1 2 3	

63. Echoes phrases that others say to him/her	0 1 2 3	
64. Excess weight loss without being sick	0 1 2 3	
65. Excitable	0 1 2 3	
66. Fails to finish things he/she starts	0 1 2 3	
67. Fears certain animal, places, or situations other than school (give details): _____	0 1 2 3	
68. Fears going to school	0 1 2 3	
69. Fears he/she might do something bad	0 1 2 3	
70. Feelings are easily hurt	0 1 2 3	
71. Feels he/she can't succeed	0 1 2 3	
72. Feels he/she has to be perfect	0 1 2 3	
73. Feels or complains that no one loves him/her	0 1 2 3	
74. Feels too guilty	0 1 2 3	
75. Feels worthless or inferior	0 1 2 3	
76. Generally seems odd or peculiar	0 1 2 3	
77. Gets angry if routines are disrupted	0 1 2 3	
78. Gets hurt a lot; accident-prone	0 1 2 3	
79. Gets into everything	0 1 2 3	
80. Gets picked on by other kids	0 1 2 3	
81. Gets teased a lot	0 1 2 3	
82. Goes on eating binges	0 1 2 3	
83. Hangs around kids who get in trouble	0 1 2 3	
84. Has a hard time making friends	0 1 2 3	
85. Has difficulty making conversation with other kids	0 1 2 3	
86. Has trouble following directions	0 1 2 3	
87. Has trouble getting to sleep	0 1 2 3	
88. Hears things that aren't there (give details): _____	0 1 2 3	
89. Hits others	0 1 2 3	
90. Hums or makes odd noises	0 1 2 3	
91. Ignored by other kids	0 1 2 3	
92. Impulsive or acts without thinking	0 1 2 3	
93. Insensitive to others' pain	0 1 2 3	
94. Insists that certain things always be done in the same order (give details): _____	0 1 2 3	
95. Involved in sex play with others	0 1 2 3	
96. Irritable	0 1 2 3	
97. Is a perfectionist; gets upset if everything is not exactly right	0 1 2 3	
98. Is dangerously daring	0 1 2 3	
99. Is preoccupied with "dirty" pictures or stories	0 1 2 3	
100. Lacks self-confidence	0 1 2 3	
101. Lies	0 1 2 3	
102. Looks unhappy without good reason	0 1 2 3	
103. Loses train of thought	0 1 2 3	
104. Loss of ability to have fun	0 1 2 3	
105. Loud	0 1 2 3	
106. Makes repetitious movements	0 1 2 3	
107. Mumbles instead of speaking clearly	0 1 2 3	
108. Needs constant supervision	0 1 2 3	
109. Nervous movements or twitching	0 1 2 3	
110. Nervous, highstrung, or tense	0 1 2 3	
111. Nightmares	0 1 2 3	
112. No interest in making friends	0 1 2 3	
113. Not liked by other kids	0 1 2 3	
114. Overactive	0 1 2 3	
115. Overeating	0 1 2 3	
116. Overtired	0 1 2 3	
117. Overweight	0 1 2 3	
118. Passive or lacks initiative	0 1 2 3	
119. Persists and nags; can't take no for an answer	0 1 2 3	
120. Physically attacks people	0 1 2 3	
121. Picks nose, skin, or other parts of body	0 1 2 3	
122. Picks on younger kids	0 1 2 3	
123. Plays with own sex parts in public	0 1 2 3	

Please see other side

124. Plays with own sex parts too much	0 1 2 3	
125. Poor school work	0 1 2 3	
126. Poorly coordinated or clumsy	0 1 2 3	
127. Prefers to be alone	0 1 2 3	
128. Problems with eyes, other than those corrected by glasses (give details): _____		
	0 1 2 3	
129. Pulls at the hands or clothes of adults	0 1 2 3	
130. Punishment doesn't change his/her behavior	0 1 2 3	
131. Quickly shifts from one activity to another	0 1 2 3	
132. Rapid shifts between sadness and excitement	0 1 2 3	
133. Rashes or other skin problems without known medical cause (give details): _____		
	0 1 2 3	
134. Refuses to eat	0 1 2 3	
135. Refuses to talk in certain situations	0 1 2 3	
136. Repeats certain acts over and over (give details): __		
	0 1 2 3	
137. Repeats certain words or phrases over and over	0 1 2 3	
138. Resists going to school	0 1 2 3	
139. Restless movements during sleep	0 1 2 3	
140. Runs away from home	0 1 2 3	
141. Sad or depressed	0 1 2 3	
142. Says strange things or expresses strange ideas (give details):_____		
	0 1 2 3	
143. Says things that don't make sense	0 1 2 3	
144. Screams	0 1 2 3	
145. Secretive, keeps things to self	0 1 2 3	
146. Seems to need to touch everything	0 1 2 3	
147. Seems to think others are out to get him/her	0 1 2 3	
148. Seems unable to tell the difference between imaginary and real things or events	0 1 2 3	
149. Sees things that aren't there (give details:) _____		
	0 1 2 3	
150. Self-conscious or easily embarrassed	0 1 2 3	
151. Selfish or won't share	0 1 2 3	
152. Sets fires	0 1 2 3	
153. Sexual problems (give details): _____		
	0 1 2 3	
154. Shows fear of strangers	0 1 2 3	
155. Shows little affection toward people	0 1 2 3	
156. Shows little interest in things around him/her	0 1 2 3	
157. Shows no fear of getting hurt	0 1 2 3	
158. Shows off or clowns	0 1 2 3	
159. Shows panic for no good reason	0 1 2 3	
160. Shy or timid	0 1 2 3	
161. Sleeps less than most kids his/her age	0 1 2 3	
162. Sleeps more than most kids during the day and/or night	0 1 2 3	
163. Smokes tobacco	0 1 2 3	
164. Sniffs at things as if they smelled	0 1 2 3	
165. Speaks in short sentences or single words	0 1 2 3	
166. Speech is hard to understand	0 1 2 3	
167. Speech problems (give details): _____		
	0 1 2 3	
168. Stares into space or seems preoccupied	0 1 2 3	
169. Starts fights	0 1 2 3	
170. Stays out late at night	0 1 2 3	
171. Stays with adults to avoid other kids	0 1 2 3	
172. Steals at home	0 1 2 3	
173. Steals directly from people (purse snatching, mugging, etc.)	0 1 2 3	
174. Steals outside home in a sneaky way (shoplifting, bike snatching, etc.)	0 1 2 3	
175. Stores up things he/she doesn't need	0 1 2 3	
176. Strange behavior (give details): _____		
	0 1 2 3	
177. Stubborn	0 1 2 3	
178. Sucks thumb	0 1 2 3	
179. Sudden changes in mood or feelings	0 1 2 3	
180. Sulks	0 1 2 3	
181. Suspicious of others	0 1 2 3	
182. Swears or uses obscene language	0 1 2 3	
183. Talks about killing self	0 1 2 3	
184. Talks or cries out in sleep	0 1 2 3	
185. Talks or thinks about sex too much	0 1 2 3	
186. Talks too much	0 1 2 3	
187. Teases other kids	0 1 2 3	
188. Temper tantrums or hot temper	0 1 2 3	
189. Thinks self too fat despite normal weight	0 1 2 3	
190. Threatens people	0 1 2 3	
191. Too concerned about own health	0 1 2 3	
192. Too concerned with neatness or cleanliness	0 1 2 3	
193. Too fearful or anxious	0 1 2 3	
194. Truant, skips school	0 1 2 3	
195. Uncooperative	0 1 2 3	
196. Underactive, slow-moving, or lacks energy	0 1 2 3	
197. Unusually curious about sex	0 1 2 3	
198. Unusually messy or sloppy	0 1 2 3	
199. Unusually preoccupied with gore and violence	0 1 2 3	
200. Uses alcohol without parents' approval	0 1 2 3	
201. Uses drugs for non-medical purposes (give details): _____		
	0 1 2 3	
202. Vandalizes property with others	0 1 2 3	
203. Vomits, throws up (without medical cause)	0 1 2 3	
204. Wakes up often at night	0 1 2 3	
205. Wakes up too early in the morning	0 1 2 3	
206. Wets self during the day	0 1 2 3	
207. Wets the bed	0 1 2 3	
208. Whines	0 1 2 3	
209. Wishes to be of opposite sex	0 1 2 3	
210. Withdrawn, doesn't get involved with others	0 1 2 3	
211. Won't stick up for self	0 1 2 3	
212. Worries	0 1 2 3	
213. Would rather play with older kids than with kids his/her age	0 1 2 3	
214. Would rather play with younger kids than with kids his/her age	0 1 2 3	
215. Writes odd words or phrases on schoolwork, in books, etc.	0 1 2 3	
216. Please add any other problems your child has.		
_____	0 1 2 3	
_____	0 1 2 3	
_____	0 1 2 3	
_____	0 1 2 3	

Please be sure you have answered all items

XI.   Feel free to add any additional comments that will help in understanding your child _____

_____

_____

TABLE B1

CALCULATION OF SOCIAL COMPETENCE SCORES

	As Separate Items	When Combining
Activities scale:		
I. Sports:		
A. Number of sports	$0-4^a$	$0-2^b$
B. Mean time in sports	$0-2^c$	$\left.\right\} 0-2^d$
C. Mean skill in sports	$0-2^c$	
II. Hobbies and activities:		
A. Number of activities	$0-4^a$	$0-2^b$
B. Mean time in activities	$0-2^c$	$\left.\right\} 0-2^d$
C. Mean skill in activities	$0-2^c$	
III. Jobs:		
A. Number of jobs	$0-4^a$	$0-2^b$
B. Mean skill in jobs	$0-2^c$	$0-2^c$
Activities scale score		$0-12^e$
Social scale:		
IV. Organizations:		
A. Number of organizations	$0-4^a$	$0-2^b$
B. Mean participation in organizations	$0-2^c$	$0-2^c$
V. Friendships:		
A. Number of friends	$0-3^f$	$0-2^g$
B. Contacts with friends	$0-2^h$	$0-2^h$
VI. Get-along-with items:		
A. Siblings	$0-2^{i,j}$	
B. Peers	$0-2^i$	$\left.\right\} 0-2^k$
C. Parents	$0-2^i$	
D. Work alone	$0-2^i$	$\left.\right\} 0-2^l$
E. Play alone	$0-2^i$	
Social scale score		$0-12^e$

TABLE B1 (*Continued*)

	As Separate Items	When Combining
School scale:		
VIIA. Mean academic performance	$0-4^{m}$	$0-3^{n}$
VIIB. (No) Special class	$0-1^{o}$	$0-1^{o}$
VIIC. (No) Grade repetition	$0-1^{o}$	$0-1^{o}$
VIID. (No) Academic problems	$0-1^{o}$	$0-1^{o}$
School scale score		$0-6^{p}$
VIII. Best things about child	$0-1^{q}$	
IX. Concerns about child	$0-1^{r}$	
Total Social Competence score		$0-30^{s}$

Note.—The first column indicates the range of possible scores when the ACQ item was scored to produce the 23 competence items used in ANCOVAs and discriminant analyses. The second column indicates the range of possible scores when the scoring was modified before the subitems were summed to produce scale scores and the Total Social Competence score. These modifications made the scale scores comparable to those of the CBCL. All means were rounded to .5.

[a] Number of sports, hobbies and activities, jobs, and organizations was scored as the number listed.

[b] For number of sports, hobbies and activities, jobs, and organizations: if 0 or 1 sports etc. were listed, it was scored as 0; 2 sports were scored as 1; 3 or 4 sports were scored as 2 (i.e., both ends of scale collapsed).

[c] For mean time and skill ratings of sports, hobbies and activities, jobs, and organizations: "don't know" was scored as missing; "less than average" = 0; "average" = 1; "more than/above average" = 2.

[d] When combining into the Activities scale, separate mean ratings for time and for skill were combined into a single mean time and skill.

[e] Sum of preceding six items (in second column). If one of the six items was missing, the mean of the other five was substituted; if more than one item was missing, the total scale score was missing.

[f] For number of friends: "none" = 0; "1" = 1; "2 or 3" = 2; "4 or more" = 3.

[g] For number of friends: "none" or "1" = 0; "2 or 3" = 1; "4 or more" = 2 (i.e., bottom end of scale collapsed).

[h] For contacts with friends: if VA. (number of friends) was listed as "none" or if VB. (contacts with friends) was listed as "less than 1" = 0; "1 or 2" = 1; "3 or more" = 2.

[i] For get-along-with items: "worse" = 0; "about average" = 1; "better" = 2.

[j] "Has no brothers or sisters" = missing.

[k] Siblings, peers, and parents averaged into one score.

[l] Works and plays alone averaged into one score.

[m] For each academic subject: "failing" = 0; "below average" = 1; "average" = 2; "above average" = 3; "far above average" = 4. After nonacademic subjects listed in error were excluded, a single average for all academic subjects was computed. If the child was younger than 6 years old, or if "does not go to school" was checked, then this mean was scored as missing.

[n] For each academic subject: "failing" = 0; "below average" = 1; "average" = 2; "above average" or "far above average" = 3 (i.e., top end of scale collapsed). The mean was taken as in n. m above.

[o] "Yes" = 0; "no" = 1. (Although this may seem backward, we were constructing a scale of competence, so the absence of these problems was scored to reflect greater competence.)

[p] Sum of the preceding four items (in second column). Missing if child was younger than 6 years old or if any of the four subitems was missing.

[q] Scored 0 if nothing positive was listed about the child, 1 if anything positive was listed.

[r] Scored 0 if anything negative was listed about the child, 1 if nothing negative was listed.

[s] Sum of Activities, Social, and School scale scores. Calculated only if all three scale scores were present and child was 6 years or older. (Children younger than 6 had a Total Competence score based on only the Activities and Social scale scores.)

ISR Institute for Survey Research

Temple University • 1601 N. Broad Street • Philadelphia, Pa. 19122 • Phone (215) 787-8355

Leonard LoSciuto, Ph. D.
Director

Dear Parent:

The United States Public Health Service is supporting a national survey of children's behavior, as reported by their parents. The survey is being conducted by Temple University's Institute for Survey Research.

Interviewers are visiting a random sample of families throughout the U.S. Your family is one of them -- no other family can be substituted for yours. Only you may answer for all the families you represent. Your participation in this important survey is completely voluntary and essential for its success.

Your interviewer carries an identification card with his or her name on it. This card means that he or she has been trained and is authorized to conduct interviews for the Institute for Survey Research and that he or she will keep all information confidential.

As part of a nationwide evaluation of the ACQ Behavior Checklist, your responses will be coded in anonymous form and pooled with the responses of parents all around the country for statistical analysis. Neither your name nor the name of your child will be included in the materials to be analyzed.

The value of this study depends on the willingness of each chosen parent to participate. If you have any questions, your interviewer should be able to answer them. If not, please call me.

Thank you for your help.

Sincerely,

Ellin Spector

Ellin Spector
Study Director

1. In this household, what is the total number of adults, including yourself, related to the study child?
2. What is the total number of adults not related to the study child?
3. Including the study child, what is the total number of children in this household?
4. Are you presently married to the child's [father/mother]?
5. Were you ever married to the child's [father/mother]?
6. How did that marriage end? Were you (1) separated; (2) divorced; (3) widowed; or (4) what _____?
7. Are you presently (1) married to someone other than the child's parent; (2) in a common-law marriage to someone other than the child's parent; (3) living with a partner of the opposite sex who is the child's parent; (4) living with a partner of the opposite sex who is not the child's parent; (5) separated; (6) divorced; (7) widowed; or (8) have you never been married?
8. Are you the child's (1) biological; (2) adoptive; (3) step-; or (4) foster parent?
9. Is your [husband/wife] the child's (1) biological; (2) adoptive; (3) step-; or (4) foster parent?
10. Besides you, who, if anyone, in the home regularly cares for the child? (1) relative; (2) nonrelative; (3) no one.
11. About how many hours a week is the child cared for by a [relative/nonrelative] in your home?
12. Who, if anyone, outside your home regularly cares for the child? (1) relative; (2) nonrelative; (3) no one.
13. About how many hours a week is the child cared for by a [relative/nonrelative] outside your home?
14. About how many other children are cared for with your child outside your home?

15. Please look at this card and tell me the total income that you and all other members of your household had before taxes last year, 1985. Include everyone's income from all sources—wages, salaries, social security, retirement benefits, money from relatives, rent from property, and so forth. You can just give me the letter from this card for the weekly, monthly, or yearly amount of total income for the entire household.

Weekly	Monthly	Yearly	(Circle Number)
$96 or less	$417 or less	Under $5,000	A 01
$97–$192	$418–$750	$5,000–$9,999	B 02
$193–$288	$751–$1,250	$10,000–$14,999	C 03
$289–$385	$1,251–$1,667	$15,000–$19,999	D 04
$386–$480	$1,668–$2,083	$20,000–$24,999	E 05
$481–$673	$2,084–$2,917	$25,000–$34,999	F 06
$674–$961	$2,918–$4,167	$35,000–$49,999	G 07
$962–$1,442	$4,168–$6,250	$50,000–$74,999	H 08
$1,443 or more	$6,251 or more	$75,000 or more	I 09

16. Does anyone in this household receive assistance through (1) the Aid to Families with Dependent Children Program, sometimes called AFDC or ADC; (2) WIC; (3) foodstamps; (4) unemployment insurance; (5) any other government assistance?
17. Has anyone in this household, including the child, or anyone related to the child, received mental health services from a psychiatrist, psychologist, social worker, or guidance clinic?
18. What is that person's relationship to the child?
19. What was the illness or disorder called?
20. Did [he/she] go for treatment at an office, or was [he/she] hospitalized?
21. When was the last time the child was treated?

INFORMATION FOR PARENTS COMPLETING THE ACQ IN CLINICAL SETTINGS

Because parents usually know the most about their child, we would like you to fill out the ACQ Behavior Checklist to describe your child's behavior.

We will use this information as part of our evaluation of your child. In addition, as part of a nationwide evaluation of the ACQ Checklist, your responses will be coded in anonymous form and pooled with the responses of parents all around the country for statistical analysis. Neither your name nor your child's name will be included in the materials to be analyzed.

Because we are especially interested in parents' views, we would appreciate any additional comments you care to write on the ACQ Behavior Checklist. If an item seems unclear, for example, please write down what you think is wrong with it.

If you have questions, please ask the person who gave you the form to fill out.

Many thanks for your help.

CLINICAL SERVICES THAT SUPPLIED ACQS FOR REFERRED CHILDREN

University of Arkansas Child Study Center
Downstate Medical Center, New York City
University of Iowa Pediatric Department
Maine Medical Center, Portland
Mid-Missouri Mental Health Center, Columbia
University of Minnesota Child Psychiatry
Morristown, NJ, Memorial Hospital
University of New Mexico BCMH/MRC Programs for Children
Medical College of Ohio
Oregon Health Sciences University
Seattle Children's Orthopedic Hospital
University of South Carolina School of Medicine
Stanford University
University of Vermont Center for Children, Youth, and Families
Washburn Clinic, Minneapolis
Washington, DC, Children's Hospital
Wilder Foundation, St. Paul, MN
Worcester, MA, Youth Guidance Center

TABLE G1

PERCENTAGE OF VARIANCE ACCOUNTED FOR BY SIGNIFICANT ($p < .01$) EFFECTS ON
BEHAVIORAL/EMOTIONAL PROBLEMS

ITEM[a]	CLINICAL STATUS[b]	SEX[c]	AGE[d]	INTERACTIONS[e] C × S	INTERACTIONS[e] C × A	COVARIATE SES[f]
1. Absentminded or forgets easily	6	$<1^M$	2^O	...	<1	...
2. Acts like opposite sex (5)	...	1^F	1^Y	<1	...	...
3. Acts silly or giggles too much	...	$<1^F$	2^Y	<1	...	...
4. Acts spitefully	6	...	$<1^Y$	...	...	<1
5. Acts too young for his/her age (1)	8	$<1^M$	$<1^{NL}$	...	...	...
6. Admires people who break the law	4	$<1^M$	2^O	<1	1	$<1^g$
7. Admires tough guys ..	2	10^M	...	<1	<1	<1
8. Afraid of making a mistake	1	...	2^{NL}	...	...	$<1^U$
9. Afraid to try new things	5	...	...	...	...	$<1^U$
10. Always on the go	$<1^{N,g}$	1^M	3^Y	$<1^g$	...	...
11. Argues (3)[E]	7	$<1^M$	...	...	...	...
12. Angry moods	11	...	$<1^{NL,g}$	...	<1	...
13. Avoids looking others in the eye	9	$<1^M$	$<1^{NL,g}$	...	<1	<1
14. Bites fingernails (44) ..	2	$<1^F$	$<1^{NL}$	...	...	<1
15. Blames others for own mistakes or problems	9	$<1^M$	$<1^{NL}$	...	<1	...
16. Bossy	4	$<1^F$	$<1^Y$	...	...	...
17. Bowel movements outside toilet (6)	2	$<1^M$	2^Y	<1	<1	$<1^g$
18. Brags, boasts (7)[E]	1	3^M	$<1^{NL}$	...	<1	...
19. Bullies or is mean to others (16)[E]	7	$<1^M$	$<1^Y$	$<1^g$	...	<1
20. Can't concentrate, can't pay attention for long (8)	18	2^M	$<1^{NL}$	<1	...	...

ITEM[a]	CLINICAL STATUS[b]	SEX[c]	AGE[d]	INTERACTIONS[e]		COVARIATE SES[f]
				C × S	C × A	
21. Can't get mind off certain thoughts (9)	6	...	...	...	< 1	...
22. Can't make up mind or make choices	5	...	< 1^{NL}	...	...	...
23. Can't sit still, squirms, or fidgets (10^h)	5	2^M	5^Y	< 1	...	< 1
24. Can't stand having things out of place ...	< $1^{N,g}$	...	...	...	...	...
25. Can't stand waiting; wants everything now	5	< 1^M	1^Y	...	...	< 1^g
26. Cheats ($43^h)^E$	6	< 1^M	...	...	< 1	< 1
27. Clings to adults or is too dependent (11) ...	4	< 1^F	3^Y	< 1	...	< 1
28. Complains too much ..	6	...	< 1^{NL}	...	...	...
29. Complains of aches or pains in arms or legs $(56a)^I$	3	< 1^F	...	...	...	...
30. Complains of dizziness $(51)^I$	2	< 1^F	2^O	< 1	< 1	< 1^g
31. Complains of headaches $(56b)^I$	4	< 1^F	2^O	< 1	< 1	< 1
32. Complains of loneliness $(12)^I$	4	< 1^F	< 1^Y	...	< 1	...
33. Complains of nausea or feeling sick $(56c)^I$ ..	4	< 1^F	< 1^{NL}	< 1	< 1	< 1
34. Complains of stomach aches or cramps $(56f)^I$	4	1^F	< 1^{NL}	< 1	< 1	...
35. Confused or seems to be in a fog (13)	8	...	< 1^O	...	< 1	...
36. Constantly asks for help	7	...	4^Y	...	...	< 1^g
37. Constipated, doesn't move bowels (49)	1	...	...	...	...	...
38. Cries without good reason $(14)^I$	5	< 1^F	4^Y	< 1	< 1	< 1
39. Cruel to animals (15)	3	< 1^M	1^Y	< 1	...	< 1
40. Day-dreams or gets lost in his/her thoughts (17)	5	< 1^M	1^O	...	< 1^g	...
41. Defiant	12	< 1^M	< 1^Y	...	...	...
42. Deliberately annoys others	8	2^M	< 1^Y	< 1	...	...
43. Deliberately destroys things belonging to others $(21)^E$	7	1^M	< 1^Y	< 1	...	< 1
44. Deliberately harms self or attempts suicide (18)	4	< 1^F	< 1^O	< 1	< 1	< 1
45. Deliberately hurts other kids	6	< 1^M	1^Y	< 1	< 1	< 1

Item[a]	Clinical Status[b]	Sex[c]	Age[d]	Interactions[e] C × S	Interactions[e] C × A	Covariate SES[f]
46. Deliberately tries to vomit	< 1	. . .	. . .	< 1	. . .	. . .
47. Demands attention (19)[E]	9	. . .	4[Y]	. . .	. . .	. . .
48. Destroys his/her own things (20)[E]	8	2[M]	2[Y]	< 1	. . .	< 1
49. Diarrhea or loose bowels	1	. . .	. . .	. . .	. . .	. . .
50. Disobedient at home (22)[E]	15	< 1[M]	1[Y]	. . .	. . .	. . .
51. Disobedient at school (23)[E]	13	3[M]	< 1[NL]	< 1	. . .	< 1
52. Does things slowly and incorrectly	10	< 1[M]	< 1[NL]	. . .	< 1	< 1
53. Doesn't answer when people talk to him/her	9	< 1[M]	1[Y]	. . .	. . .	< 1
54. Doesn't get along with other kids (25)	12	< 1[M]	< 1[Y]	< 1	< 1	. . .
55. Doesn't seem to feel guilty after misbehaving (26)[E]	11	< 1[M]	. . .	. . .	< 1[g]	< 1
56. Doesn't want to go out of home	3	. . .	< 1[O]	. . .	< 1	. . .
57. Dresses like or plays at being opposite sex	< 1[g]	. . .	1[Y]	. . .	< 1	. . .
58. Drowsy, sleepy	4	. . .	3[O]	. . .	1	. . .
59. Easily distracted	13	2[M]	1[Y]	< 1	< 1	. . .
60. Easily flustered around other people	8	. . .	. . .	. . .	. . .	< 1
61. Easily jealous (27)[E] . . .	7	< 1[F]	1[Y]	. . .	. . .	< 1
62. Eats or drinks things that are not food (28)	1	. . .	. . .	. . .	. . .	. . .
63. Echoes phrases that others say to him/her	< 1	< 1[M]	4[Y]	. . .	. . .	. . .
64. Excess weight loss without being sick	1	< 1[F]	< 1[O]	< 1	< 1	. . .
65. Excitable	5	< 1[M]	3[Y]	< 1	. . .	. . .
66. Fails to finish things he/she starts	12	< 1[M]	< 1[NL,g]	< 1	< 1	. . .
67. Fears certain animals, places, or situations other than school (29)	1	< 1[F]	3[Y]	. . .	. . .	. . .
68. Fears going to school (30)	6	. . .	< 1[O]	. . .	< 1	< 1
69. Fears he/she might do something bad (31)[I] . .	3	. . .	. . .	. . .	. . .	. . .
70. Feelings are easily hurt	5	< 1[F]	< 1[Y]	. . .	< 1	< 1
71. Feels he/she can't succeed	13	. . .	3[O]	. . .	1	. . .

ITEM[a]	CLINICAL STATUS[b]	SEX[c]	AGE[d]	INTERACTIONS[e] C × S	INTERACTIONS[e] C × A	COVARIATE SES[f]
72. Feels he/she has to be perfect (32)[I]	< 1	...	1^O	...	...	$< 1^U$
73. Feels or complains that no one loves him/her (33)[I]	8	$< 1^F$	1^{NL}	...	< 1	< 1
74. Feels too guilty (52)[I] ..	4	$< 1^{F,g}$	$< 1^O$	...	< 1	...
75. Feels worthless or inferior (35)[I]	13	...	4°	...	2	$< 1^U$
76. Generally seems odd or peculiar	6	...	$< 1^O$	...	< 1	< 1
77. Gets angry if routines are disrupted	4	$< 1^M$	...	...	...	< 1
78. Gets hurt a lot; accident-prone (36) ...	3	...	1^Y	...	...	...
79. Gets into everything ..	4	1^M	5^Y	< 1	...	< 1
80. Gets picked on by other kids	6	$< 1^M$	3^Y	...	< 1	< 1
81. Gets teased a lot (38)	5	$< 1^M$	2^Y	< 1	< 1	< 1
82. Goes on eating binges	1	$< 1^F$	1^O	...	$< 1^g$	< 1
83. Hangs around kids who get in trouble (39)[E]	7	$< 1^M$	3°	< 1	2	< 1
84. Has a hard time making friends	12	$< 1^M$	1^O	< 1	< 1	...
85. Has difficulty making conversation with other kids	7	...	...	...	$< 1^g$	...
86. Has trouble following directions	15	$< 1^M$	$< 1^Y$	< 1	< 1	...
87. Has trouble getting to sleep (100[h])	8	...	$< 1^{NL,g}$	...	...	...
88. Hears things that aren't there (40)	1	...	...	...	...	< 1
89. Hits others	7	2^M	4^Y	< 1	...	< 1
90. Hums or makes odd noises	1	1^M	1^Y	...	...	< 1
91. Ignored by other kids	6	$< 1^M$	$< 1^{NL}$	< 1	< 1	< 1
92. Impulsive or acts without thinking (41)	11	1^M	...	< 1	...	...
93. Insensitive to others' pain	4	$< 1^M$	...	< 1	...	...
94. Insists that certain things always be done in the same order	...	...	1^Y	...	...	...
95. Involved in sex play with others	3	...	$< 1^{NL}$	...	...	...
96. Irritable (86[h])[E]	11	...	$< 1^O$	...	< 1	...
97. Is a perfectionist; gets upset if everything is not exactly right	$< 1^g$	...	$< 1^Y$	...	...	...
98. Is dangerously daring	2	2^M	$< 1^Y$	...	...	< 1

Item[a]	Clinical Status[b]	Sex[c]	Age[d]	Interactions[e]		Covariate SES[f]
				C × S	C × A	
99. Is preoccupied with "dirty" pictures or stories	2	$< 1^M$	$< 1^O$	. . .	. . .	. . .
100. Lacks self-confidence	17	. . .	3°	. . .	1	. . .
101. Lies (43[h])[E]	13	$< 1^M$	. . .	. . .	1	< 1
102. Looks unhappy without good reason (103[h])[I]	13	$< 1^F$	1^O	. . .	< 1	< 1
103. Loses train of thought	10	$< 1^M$	$< 1^{NL}$	. . .	< 1	< 1
104. Loss of ability to have fun	10	. . .	1^O	. . .	< 1	. . .
105. Loud (104)[E]	4	$< 1^M$	4^Y	. . .	. . .	< 1
106. Makes repetitious movements	3	$< 1^M$	. . .	. . .	. . .	< 1
107. Mumbles instead of speaking clearly	4	$< 1^M$	. . .	. . .	. . .	< 1
108. Needs constant supervision	12	$< 1^M$	$< 1^Y$	< 1	. . .	< 1
109. Nervous movements or twitching (46)	6	$< 1^M$	. . .	. . .	. . .	< 1
110. Nervous, highstrung, or tense (45)[I]	14	$< 1^M$	$< 1^O$	< 1	. . .	< 1
111. Nightmares (47)	5	$< 1^F$	2^Y	. . .	. . .	. . .
112. No interest in making friends	6	. . .	$< 1^O$	. . .	< 1	< 1
113. Not liked by other kids (48)	10	$< 1^M$	1^{NL}	< 1	. . .	. . .
114. Overactive (10[h])	5	2^M	3^Y	< 1	< 1	< 1
115. Overeating (53)	2	. . .	1^O	. . .	. . .	< 1
116. Overtired (54)[I]	5	. . .	2^O	. . .	< 1	. . .
117. Overweight (55)	< 1	$< 1^F$	2^O	. . .	. . .	. . .
118. Passive or lacks initiative	10	$< 1^M$	4°	. . .	2	. . .
119. Persists and nags; can't take no for an answer	9	$< 1^M$	$< 1^Y$	. . .	. . .	$< 1^U$
120. Physically attacks people (57)[E]	7	$< 1^M$	$< 1^Y$	< 1	. . .	< 1
121. Picks nose, skin, or other parts of body (58)	4	. . .	2^Y	. . .	. . .	. . .
122. Picks on younger kids	3	$< 1^M$	. . .	. . .	. . .	< 1
123. Plays with own sex parts in public (59) . . .	< 1	. . .	2^Y	. . .	< 1	. . .
124. Plays with own sex parts too much (60) . . .	3	$< 1^{M,g}$	2^Y	. . .	< 1	. . .
125. Poor school work (61)	19	1^M	7°	< 1	2	< 1
126. Poorly coordinated or clumsy (62)	6	. . .	. . .	. . .	. . .	. . .
127. Prefers to be alone (42)[I]	4	. . .	2^O	. . .	1	. . .
128. Problems with eyes, other than those corrected by glasses (56d)[I]	1	. . .	. . .	. . .	. . .	< 1

Item[a]	Clinical Status[b]	Sex[c]	Age[d]	Interactions[e] C × S	C × A	Covariate SES[f]
129. Pulls at the hands or clothes of adults	3	...	9^Y	...	< 1	...
130. Punishment doesn't change his/her be-havior	17	$< 1^M$	...	...	...	< 1
131. Quickly shifts from one activity to another	6	$< 1^M$	3^Y	$< 1^g$	...	< 1
132. Rapid shifts between sadness and ex-citement	9	$< 1^F$	...	...	...	< 1
133. Rashes or other skin problems without known medical cause $(56e)^I$	< 1	...	...	...	...	...
134. Refuses to eat (24)	3	$< 1^{F,g}$	3^Y	< 1	...	< 1
135. Refuses to talk in cer-tain situations $(65)^I$	9	...	$< 1^{NL}$	...	< 1	< 1
136. Repeats certain acts over and over (66)	3	...	$< 1^Y$	...	$< 1^g$	< 1
137. Repeats certain words or phrases over and over	1	$< 1^M$	2^Y	...	...	< 1
138. Resists going to school	8	...	2^O	...	2	< 1
139. Restless movements during sleep	4	...	$< 1^Y$	...	...	< 1
140. Runs away from home $(67)^E$	5	...	2^O	...	2	...
141. Sad or depressed $(103^h)^I$	15	$< 1^F$	3°	< 1	2	...
142. Says strange things or expresses strange ideas (85)	4	...	...	...	...	< 1
143. Says things that don't make sense	3	...	$< 1^Y$	< 1	...	1
144. Screams $(68)^E$	4	$< 1^F$	4^Y	...	...	< 1
145. Secretive, keeps things to self $(69)^I$	8	...	5°	...	< 1	< 1
146. Seems to need to touch everything	5	$< 1^M$	5^Y	...	...	< 1
147. Seems to think others are out to get him/her $(34)^I$	9	$< 1^M$	2^O	...	1	< 1
148. Seems unable to tell the difference between imaginary and real things or events	4	...	$< 1^Y$	...	...	< 1
149. See things that aren't there (70)	1	$< 1^F$	$< 1^{NL}$	$< 1^g$	...	...
150. Self-conscious or easily embarrassed $(71)^I$	3	$< 1^F$	1^O	...	< 1	...
151. Selfish or won't share .	4	$< 1^{M,g}$	2^Y	...	...	...
152. Sets fires $(72)^E$	2	1^M	$< 1^{NL,g}$	< 1	...	< 1

TABLE G1 (*Continued*)

ITEM[a]	CLINICAL STATUS[b]	SEX[c]	AGE[d]	INTERACTIONS[e] C × S	C × A	COVARIATE SES[f]
153. Sexual problems (73)	3	$< 1^F$	...	< 1	...	< 1
154. Shows fear of strangers	...	$< 1^F$	4^Y	...	< 1	< 1
155. Shows little affection toward people	5	...	1^O	...	< 1	...
156. Shows little interest in things around him/her	5	...	1^O	...	1	< 1
157. Shows no fear of getting hurt	1	$< 1^M$	$< 1^{NL,g}$	...	...	...
158. Shows off or clowns (74)[E]	2	3^M	3^Y	< 1	...	< 1
159. Shows panic for no good reason	4	$< 1^F$	...	...	...	< 1
160. Shy or timid (75)[I]	< 1	$< 1^F$	$< 1^{Y,g}$	...	...	...
161. Sleeps less than most kids his/her age (76)	2	...	$< 1^Y$	...	...	...
162. Sleeps more than most kids during the day and/or night (77)	2	$< 1^{F,g}$	2^O	$< 1^g$	1	...
163. Smokes tobacco	3	...	9°	...	4	< 1
164. Sniffs at things as if they smelled	< 1	...	$< 1^Y$	...	...	< 1
165. Speaks in short sentences or single words	3	...	$< 1^{NL}$	...	...	< 1
166. Speech is hard to understand	3	...	1^Y	...	< 1	...
167. Speech problems (79)	3	$< 1^M$	2^Y	...	< 1	...
168. Stares into space or seems preoccupied (80)[I]	8	...	$< 1^{NL}$	...	< 1	< 1
169. Starts fights (37)[E]	7	$< 1^M$	$< 1^Y$	< 1	...	< 1
170. Stays out late at night	2	$< 1^M$	9°	...	2	< 1
171. Stays with adults to avoid other kids	5	$< 1^{F,g}$	...	...	...	< 1
172. Steals at home (81)[E]	6	$< 1^M$	1^O	$< 1^g$	< 1	< 1
173. Steals directly from people (purse snatching, mugging, etc.)	< 1	...	...	...	...	...
174. Steals outside home in a sneaky way (shoplifting, bike snatching, etc.) (82)[E]	4	$< 1^M$	...	...	...	< 1
175. Stores up things he/she doesn't need (83)	$< 1^g$	...	1^{NL}	...	< 1	< 1
176. Strange behavior (84)	5	...	...	...	$< 1^g$	< 1
177. Stubborn (86[h])	8	...	$< 1^Y$	...	...	...
178. Sucks thumb (98)	< 1	$< 1^F$	4^Y	...	...	...
179. Sudden changes in mood or feelings (87)[E]	12	$< 1^F$	$< 1^O$	< 1	...	< 1

ITEM[a]	CLINICAL STATUS[b]	SEX[c]	AGE[d]	INTERACTIONS[e]		COVARIATE SES[f]
				C × S	C × A	
180. Sulks (88)[I]	6	< 1[F]	...	< 1	< 1	< 1
181. Suspicious of others (89)[I]	4	...	< 1[O]	...	1	< 1
182. Swears or uses obscene language (90)[E]	6	2[M]	4[O]	< 1	< 1	< 1
183. Talks about killing self (91)	6	...	2[O]	...	2	...
184. Talks or cries out in sleep (92)	3	...	1[Y]	...	...	...
185. Talks or thinks about sex too much (96)[E] ...	3	...	< 1[O]	< 1	...	...
186. Talks too much (93)[E]	< 1	...	2[Y]	< 1	...	< 1
187. Teases other kids (94)[E]	3	2[M]	< 1[Y]	< 1	...	< 1
188. Temper tantrums or hot temper (95)[E]	10	< 1[M]	< 1[Y]	...	...	< 1
189. Thinks self too fat despite normal weight ...	< 1	4[F]	5[O]	< 1[g]	< 1	...
190. Threatens people (97)	7	< 1[M]	...	< 1	...	< 1
191. Too concerned with own health	1	< 1[F,g]	2[O]	...	...	...
192. Too concerned with neatness or cleanliness (99)	...	< 1[F]	< 1[O]	...	...	< 1
193. Too fearful or anxious (50)[I]	6	...	...	...	...	...
194. Truant, skips school (101)[E]	5	...	8[O]	...	5	< 1
195. Uncooperative	14	< 1[M]	< 1[NL]	...	< 1	...
196. Underactive, slow-moving, or lacks energy (102)[I]	6	< 1[F]	4[O]	< 1	2	< 1
197. Unusually curious about sex	2	...	...	...	...	< 1
198. Unusually messy or sloppy	5	...	2[O]	...	< 1	< 1
199. Unusually preoccupied with gore and violence	3	2[M]	< 1[O]	< 1	< 1[g]	< 1
200. Uses alcohol without parents' approval (105[h])[E]	2	...	8[O]	...	3	...
201. Uses drugs for non-medicinal purposes (105[h])[E]	2	...	4[O]	...	3	...
202. Vandalizes property with others (106)[E]	2	< 1[M]	...	< 1	...	< 1
203. Vomits, throws up (without medical cause) (56g)[I]	1	...	...	...	...	...
204. Wakes up often at night (100[h])	5	< 1[F]	1[Y]	...	...	< 1[g]

ITEM[a]	CLINICAL STATUS[b]	SEX[c]	AGE[d]	INTERACTIONS[e] C × S	INTERACTIONS[e] C × A	COVARIATE SES[f]
205. Wakes up too early in the morning	< 1	...	3^Y	...	...	< 1
206. Wets self during the day (107)	2	...	2^Y	...	1	...
207. Wets the bed (108) ...	2	...	5^Y	...	< 1	...
208. Whines (109)	3	$< 1^F$	13^Y	...	< 1	...
209. Wishes to be of opposite sex (110)	$< 1^g$	$< 1^F$	$< 1^Y$	...	...	...
210. Withdrawn, doesn't get involved with others (111)[I]	9	...	$< 1^O$	...	< 1	< 1
211. Won't stick up for self	3	...	$< 1^{NL}$	...	...	...
212. Worries (112)[I]	7	$< 1^F$	1^O	...	< 1	...
213. Would rather play with older kids than with kids his/her age (63)[E]	2	$< 1^M$	...	...	...	< 1
214. Would rather play with younger kids than with kids his/her age (64) ..	5	...	1^{NL}	...	< 1	...
215. Writes odd words or phrases on schoolwork, in books, etc. ...	1	...	3°	...	< 1	< 1
216. Other problems (113)	$< 1^g$	...	...	...	...	...
Withdrawn	16	...	2^O	< 1	2	< 1
Somatic Complaints	8	$< 1^F$	1^O	< 1	< 1	< 1
Anxious/Depressed	16	$< 1^F$	1^O	...	< 1	...
Social Problems	14	...	1^Y	...	< 1	< 1
Thought Problems	11	...	...	...	< 1	< 1
Attention Problems	22	1^M	$< 1^{NL}$	< 1	< 1	< 1
Delinquent Behavior	16	$< 1^M$	2^O	...	2	< 1
Aggressive Behavior	15	$< 1^M$	1^Y	< 1	...	< 1
Internalizing	18	$< 1^F$	2^O	...	1	< 1
Externalizing	17	1^M	$< 1^Y$	< 1	< 1	< 1
Externalizing minus Internalizing	...	3^M	4^Y	< 1	< 1	< 1
Total problem score	22	$< 1^M$	...	...	< 1	< 1

NOTE.—Ethnic and regional effects were minimal and are discussed in text. Numbers in table indicate percentage of variance accounted for by each independent variable and covariate where the effect was significant at $p < .01$.

[a] Numbers in parentheses refer to the numbers that counterpart items bear on the CBCL. E = Externalizing items; I = Internalizing items.

[b] Referred children had higher scores on all items except 10 and 24; N = nonreferred scored higher.

[c] F = higher scores for females; M = higher scores for males.

[d] O = higher scores for older children; Y = higher scores for younger children; NL = nonlinear age effect.

[e] C × S = clinical status × sex; C × A = clinical status × age. Other interactions were minimal and are discussed in text.

[f] All significant SES effects reflect higher scores for lower-SES children, except items 8, 9, 72, 75, 119, and Internalizing; U = upper SES scored higher.

[g] Not significant when corrected for the number of analyses.

[h] Two ACQ items have a single counterpart item on the CBCL.

REFERENCES

Achenbach, T. M. (1978). The Child Behavior Profile: 1. Boys aged 6–11. *Journal of Consulting and Clinical Psychology,* **46,** 478–488.

Achenbach, T. M. (1981). *Child Behavior Checklist for Ages 4–16.* Burlington: University of Vermont, Department of Psychiatry.

Achenbach, T. M. (1985). *Assessment and taxonomy of child and adolescent psychopathology.* Newbury Park, CA: Sage.

Achenbach, T. M. (1991a). *Integrative guide for the 1991 CBCL/4–18, YSR, and TRF profiles.* Burlington: University of Vermont, Department of Psychiatry.

Achenbach, T. M. (1991b). *Manual for the Child Behavior Checklist and 1991 Profile.* Burlington: University of Vermont, Department of Psychiatry.

Achenbach, T. M., Bird, H. R., Canino, G. J., Phares, V., Gould, M., & Rubio-Stipec, M. (1990). Epidemiological comparisons of Puerto Rican and U.S. mainland children: Parent, teacher, and self reports. *Journal of the American Academy of Child and Adolescent Psychiatry,* **29,** 84–93.

Achenbach, T. M., & Brown, J. S. (1991). *Bibliography of published studies using the Child Behavior Checklist and related materials: 1991 edition.* Burlington: University of Vermont, Department of Psychiatry.

Achenbach, T. M., Conners, C. K., & Quay, H. C. (1983). *ACQ Behavior Checklist.* Burlington: University of Vermont, Department of Psychiatry.

Achenbach, T. M., Conners, C. K., Quay, H. C., Verhulst, F. C., & Howell, C. T. (1989). Replication of empirically derived syndromes as a basis for taxonomy of child/adolescent psychopathology. *Journal of Abnormal Child Psychology,* **17,** 299–323.

Achenbach, T. M., & Edelbrock, C. (1978). The classification of child psychopathology: A review and analysis of empirical efforts. *Psychological Bulletin,* **85,** 1275–1301.

Achenbach, T. M., & Edelbrock, C. (1981). Behavioral problems and competencies reported by parents of normal and disturbed children aged four to sixteen. *Monographs of the Society for Research in Child Development,* **46**(1, Serial No. 188).

Achenbach, T. M., & Edelbrock, C. (1983). *Manual for the Child Behavior Checklist and Revised Child Behavior Profile.* Burlington: University of Vermont, Department of Psychiatry.

Achenbach, T. M., & Edelbrock, C. (1986). *Manual for the Teacher's Report Form and Teacher Version of the Child Behavior Profile.* Burlington: University of Vermont, Department of Psychiatry.

Achenbach, T. M., & Edelbrock, C. (1987). *Manual for the Youth Self-Report and Profile.* Burlington: University of Vermont, Department of Psychiatry.

Achenbach, T. M., Edelbrock, C., & Howell, C. T. (1987). Empirically based assessment of the behavioral/emotional problems of 2–3-year-old children. *Journal of Abnormal Child Psychology*, **15**, 629–650.

Achenbach, T. M., Hensley, V. R., Phares, V., & Grayson, D. (1990). Problems and competencies reported by parents of Australian and American children. *Journal of Child Psychology and Psychiatry*, **31**, 265–286.

Achenbach, T. M., McConaughy, S. H., & Howell, C. T. (1987). Child/adolescent behavioral and emotional problems: Implications of cross-informant correlations for situational specificity. *Psychological Bulletin*, **101**, 213–232.

Achenbach, T. M., Verhulst, F. C., Baron, G. D., & Akkerhuis, G. W. (1987). Epidemiological comparisons of Dutch and American children: 1. Behavioral/emotional problems and competencies reported by parents for ages 4 to 16. *Journal of the American Academy of Child and Adolescent Psychiatry*, **26**, 317–325.

American Psychiatric Association. (1980). *Diagnostic and statistical manual of mental disorders* (3d ed.). Washington, DC: American Psychiatric Press.

American Psychiatric Association. (1987). *Diagnostic and statistical manual of mental disorders* (3d ed., rev.). Washington, DC: American Psychiatric Press.

Anderson, J. C., Williams, S., McGee, R., & Silva, P. A. (1987). DSM-III disorders in preadolescent children: Prevalence in a large sample from the general population. *Archives of General Psychiatry*, **44**, 69–76.

Bird, H. R., Gould, M. S., Yager, T., Staghezza, B., & Canino, G. (1989). Risk factors for maladjustment in Puerto Rican children. *Journal of the American Academy of Child and Adolescent Psychiatry*, **28**, 847–850.

Cohen, J. (1988). *Statistical power analysis for the behavioral sciences* (2d ed.). New York: Academic.

Conners, C. K. (1978). *Parent Questionnaire*. Washington, DC: Children's Hospital National Medical Center.

Costello, E. J. (1989). Developments in child psychiatric epidemiology. *Journal of the American Academy of Child and Adolescent Psychiatry*, **28**, 836–841.

Costello, E. J., Costello, A. J., Edelbrock, C., Burns, B. J., Dulcan, M. K., Brent, D., & Janiszewski, S. (1988). DSM-III disorders in pediatric primary care: Prevalence and risk factors. *Archives of General Psychiatry*, **45**, 1107–1116.

Edelbrock, C., Costello, A. J., Dulcan, M. K., Kalas, R., & Conover, N. C. (1985). Age differences in the reliability of the psychiatric interview of the child. *Child Development*, **56**, 265–275.

Fleiss, J. L. (1981). *Statistical methods for rates and proportions* (2d ed.). New York: Wiley.

Fogelman, K. (1976). *Britain's sixteen-year-olds*. London: National Children's Bureau.

Goyette, C. H., Conners, C. K., & Ulrich, R. F. (1978). Normative data on revised Conners Parent and Teacher Rating Scales. *Journal of Abnormal Child Psychology*, **6**, 221–236.

Hollingshead, A. B. (1975). *Four factor index of social status*. Unpublished manuscript. Yale University, Department of Sociology.

Hollingshead, A. B., & Redlich, F. C. (1958). *Social class and mental illness*. New York: Wiley.

Kastrup, M. (1977). Urban-rural differences in 6-year-olds. In P. J. Graham (Ed.), *Epidemiological approaches in child psychiatry* (pp. 181–194). New York: Academic.

Langner, T. S., Gersten, J. C., McCarthy, E. D., Eisenberg, J. G., Greene, E. L., & Jameson, J. D. (1976). A screening inventory for assessing psychiatric impairment in children 6 to 18. *Journal of Consulting and Clinical Psychology*, **44**, 286–296.

Lavik, N. J. (1977). Urban-rural differences in rates of disorder. In P. J. Graham (Ed.), *Epidemiological approaches in child psychiatry* (pp. 223–251). New York: Academic.

Miller, L. C. (1967). Louisville Behavior Checklist for males, 6–12 years of age. *Psychological Reports*, **21**, 885–896.

Montenegro, H. (1983). *Salud mental del escolar: Estandarización del inventario de problemas conductuales y destrezas sociales de T. Achenbach en niños de 6 a 11 años*. Santiago, Chile: Centro de Estudios de Desarollo y Estimulacion Psicosocial.

National Center for Health Statistics. (1982). *Current estimates from the National Health Interview Survey: United States, 1981* (Vital and Health Statistics, Series 10, No. 141, DHHS Publication No. PHS 83-1569). Washington, DC: U.S. Government Printing Office.

Offord, D. R., Boyle, M. H., & Racine, Y. (1989). Ontario Child Health Study: Correlates of disorder. *Journal of the American Academy of Child and Adolescent Psychiatry*, **28**, 856–860.

Offord, D. R., Boyle, M. H., Szatmari, P., Rae-Grant, N. I., Links, P. S., Cadman, D. T., Byles, J. A., Crawford, J. W., Blum, H. M., Byrne, C., Thomas, H., & Woodward, C. A. (1987). Ontario Child Health Study: 2. Six-month prevalence of disorder and rates of service utilization. *Archives of General Psychiatry*, **44**, 832–836.

Oliver, L. I. (1974). *Parent ratings of behavioral patterns of youths 12–17 years* (DHEW Publication No. HRA 74-1619). Washington, DC: U.S. Government Printing Office.

Peterson, D. R. (1961). Behavior problems of middle childhood. *Journal of Consulting Psychology*, **25**, 205–209.

Pringle, M. K., Butler, N., & Davie, R. (1966). *11,000 seven-year-olds*. London: Longman.

Quay, H. C. (1986). Classification. In H. C. Quay & J. S. Werry (Eds.), *Psychopathological disorders of childhood* (3d ed., pp. 1–42). New York: Wiley.

Quay, H. C., & Peterson, D. R. (1975). *Manual for the Behavior Problem Checklist* (rev. ed.). Coral Gables, FL: University of Miami, Department of Psychology.

Quay, H. C., & Peterson, D. R. (1982). *Revised Behavior Problem Checklist*. Miami: University of Miami, Department of Psychology.

Quay, H. C., & Peterson, D. R. (1987). *Manual for the Revised Behavior Problem Checklist*. Coral Gables, FL: University of Miami, Department of Psychology.

Roberts, J., & Baird, J. T. (1971). *Parent ratings of behavioral patterns of children* (DHEW Publication No. HSM 72-1010). Washington, DC: U.S. Government Printing Office.

Robins, L. N. (1985). Epidemiology: Reflections on testing the validity of psychiatric interviews. *Archives of General Psychiatry*, **42**, 918–924.

Rutter, M. (1981). The city and the child. *American Journal of Orthopsychiatry*, **51**, 610–625.

Rutter, M., Cox, A., Tupling, C., Berger, M., & Yule, W. (1975). Attainment and adjustment in two geographical areas: 1. The prevalence of psychiatric disorder. *British Journal of Psychiatry*, **126**, 493–509.

Rutter, M., Tizard, J., & Whitmore, K. (1970). *Education, health and behavior*. New York: Wiley.

Sakoda, J. M., Cohen, B. H., & Beall, G. (1954). Test of significance for a series of statistical tests. *Psychological Bulletin*, **51**, 172–175.

SAS Institute. (1988). *SAS/STAT User's Guild, release 6.03 edition*. Cary, NC: SAS Institute.

Shaffer, D., Fisher, P., Piacentini, J., Schwab-Stone, M., & Wicks, J. (1989). *DISC-2*. New York: Columbia University Division of Child Psychiatry.

Snook, S. C., & Gorsuch, R. L. (1989). Component analysis versus common factor analysis: A Monte Carlo study. *Psychological Bulletin*, **106**, 148–154.

Velez, C. N., Johnson, J., & Cohen, P. (1989). A longitudinal analysis of selected risk factors for childhood psychopathology. *Journal of the American Academy of Child and Adolescent Psychiatry*, **28**, 861–864.

Verhulst, F. C., & Akkerhuis, G. W. (1986). Mental health in Dutch children: 3. Behavioral/emotional problems reported by teachers of children aged 4–12. *Acta Psychiatrica Scandinavia*, **74**(Suppl. 330).

Verhulst, F. C., Akkerhuis, G. W., & Althaus, M. (1985). Mental health in Dutch children: 1. A cross-cultural comparison. *Acta Psychiatrica Scandinavica*, **72**(Suppl. 323).

Wechsler, D. (1974). *Wechsler Intelligence Scale for Children—Revised.* New York: Psychological Corp.

Weisz, J. R., Suwanlert, S., Chaiyasit, W., Weiss, B., Achenbach, T. M., & Walter, B. R. (1987). Epidemiology of behavioral and emotional problems among Thai and American children: Parent reports for ages 6 to 11. *Journal of the American Academy of Child and Adolescent Psychiatry,* **26,** 890–897.

Woodward, C. A., Thomas, H. B., Boyle, M. H., Links, P. S., & Offord, D. R. (1989). Methodologic note for child epidemiological surveys: The effects of instructions on estimates of behavior prevalence. *Journal of Child Psychology and Psychiatry,* **30,** 919–924.

Zill, N., & Peterson, J. L. (1982, January). *Trends in the behavior and emotional well-being of U.S. children: Findings from a national survey.* Paper presented at the annual meeting of the American Association for the Advancement of Science, Washington, DC.

ACKNOWLEDGMENTS

We are grateful to Drs. Stephanie H. McConaughy and Catherine Stanger for their thorough critiques of the manuscript, to Judy Ewell for her diligent preparation of the many drafts, and to David Jacobowitz for help with the analyses. This research was supported by the Esther Katz Rosen Fund of the American Psychological Foundation and by National Institute of Mental Health grant 40305. Address correspondence to Thomas M. Achenbach, Department of Psychiatry, University of Vermont, Burlington, VT 05401-3456.

COMMENTARY

METHODOLOGICAL AND SUBSTANTIVE LESSONS

JOHN E. BATES

Three of the benchmark measures in child psychopathology research throughout the past 20 years were developed by coauthors of the present *Monograph*, Thomas M. Achenbach, C. Keith Conners, and Herbert C. Quay. At this point, Achenbach's CBCL, preeminent in much of the world, is becoming the MMPI of child assessment. In the current report, with the addition to the team of Catherine T. Howell, Achenbach et al. now describe the development of a new questionnaire, the ACQ. The *Monograph* has special relevance for those whose research focuses on developmental psychopathology, but even those whose specific interests in children's individual differences lie elsewhere may be interested in the authors' systematic approach to instrument development. At the least, that approach suggests why the authors' questionnaires have been so widely used.

Despite the benchmark status of the Achenbach, Conners, and Quay measures, no one has professed satisfaction with the state of the art in this domain of assessment. Validation for the leading child psychopathology questionnaires has been good (as it goes), but the sense remains that much additional research on the concepts and measures needs to be done. In their *Monograph*, Achenbach et al. describe the foundations of an ambitious new effort to advance the assessment of children's behavior problems. They have merged their three earlier questionnaires into the ACQ so as to tap more intensively parents' perceptions of the original questionnaires' factor syndromes. The *Monograph* summarizes a substantial portion of the ACQ's development research program.

If the reader has turned to this Commentary first and wishes to know only whether the parent-report CBCL should now be abandoned and replaced by the ACQ, not much of either the *Monograph* or what follows here needs to be read. The answer, at least for now, is no. If, however, the reader's interest in the state of the art in child behavior problem assessment is broader, including perhaps interest in the empirical and theoretical bases of the CBCL as well as the consequences of using it as an index, then the *Monograph* should be read with more care. In this Commentary, I hope to provide a framework for appreciating the present contribution of Achenbach et al. as well as to direct a few comments toward future research in this domain.

In reading the *Monograph*, one may feel overwhelmed at first by the many psychometric facts that are paraded one after the other. Soon, however, one begins to appreciate the systematic crafting of the network of relations that is presented and, indeed, the fact that one needs to attend to such a network in order to evaluate a questionnaire. Then comes a growing realization of how the details reflect a broader methodological approach and theoretical perspective. Finally, having refined and evaluated the ACQ at the most basic levels, the authors introduce a second parade of findings, this time of a more substantive and more intrinsically interesting nature. There cannot be many publications within the literature on test development that provide as much information about the properties not only of composite scales but also of each individual item. Achenbach et al. have gained the luxury of such a fine-grained presentation on the strength of their methodological rigor, especially the use of a comparatively huge and carefully recruited validation sample. Consequently, the reader gets an unusually detailed look at a partially successful prototype for the next generation of child psychopathology questionnaires.

The most striking methodological lesson for me has been the demonstration that, in a questionnaire, bigger is not necessarily better, at least on the key tests described in this report. One might have expected that the ACQ, with its longer list of items (216 vs. 118 in the CBCL) and its broader response scale (four point vs. the CBCL's three point), would be more sensitive to gradations in problems. Overall, however, the ACQ is in fact not quite as accurate at discriminating between referred and nonreferred children as the CBCL. Nor are the similarities between mother and father ratings or test and retest scores as great as with the CBCL. Researchers and clinicians have various reasons for preferring shorter questionnaires, especially the desire to limit demands made on the parents' time. It is nice for once to have psychometric support for one's preferred choice, even though the justification might not have been predicted on the basis of conventional psychometric theory.

What reasons could there be for the slight but obvious superiority of the CBCL over the ACQ? Achenbach et al. emphasize the difference in the response scale. Their analyses suggest that the four-point scale elicits a narrower range of responses on a given item than the three-point scale of the CBCL. Both clinical and nonclinical group parents rated fewer ACQ items at either extreme of the scale than in comparable research on the CBCL. The nonclinical parents were especially likely to give fewer bottom-of-the-scale ratings, while the clinical parents were especially likely to give fewer high-end ratings, thus shrinking the differences in scores between the clinical and the nonclinical groups. The reduced effect size could be due to words used to describe the extremes; for example, in the four-point scale 0 = "Never or not at all true," whereas in the three-point scale 0 = "Not true." It could also be due to a more general preference for the middle ranges of a rating scale. On the other hand, the shrinking clinic versus nonclinic effect could be due in some way to the greater numbers of items; for example, perhaps there is cancellation of effects at the item level because, with more items, parents are able to shade their descriptions of their children more finely. Or, finally, it might even have something to do with the different sample sizes in the ACQ and the CBCL studies. In my own research, I have often noticed a shrinkage of effect sizes as the numbers of subjects increased, as in adding a second cohort's data to that of the first. Other researchers have informally confirmed my observation. The present ACQ study had twice as many subjects as the CBCL study with which it is compared.

Despite these speculations about the ACQ's reduced discriminative power, however, I would also suggest that the reduction of power is not completely established. For example, if the descriptions of the children are actually more finely differentiated with the extra items and broader rating scale, perhaps this will show up when the ACQ is related to a finer criterion measure than clinic versus nonclinic status or when long-term continuity versus change in adjustment is the issue. Achenbach et al. indicate that such analyses will soon be forthcoming.

Another of the methodologically interesting analyses included in the *Monograph* is that of the predictive properties of a variety of possible measures of socioeconomic status. I have never seen as systematic an exploration of commonly used indexes of social class in relation to the domain of child behavior problems. In the end, the authors conclude that the simplest among them, parent occupational status, is most worthy of being used—and so once again we are provided with an empirical justification for choosing an easier option.

It should be noted that the ACQ was purposely designed so as to maintain a link to the CBCL and that the emphasis in its refinement was on creating factor scales that are replicated across ages, across gender, and across informants (see Achenbach, Conners, Quay, Verhulst, & Howell, 1989). This means that, although the ACQ contains a remarkably broad range of items and scales, these still do not necessarily represent the full range of characteristics that parents or other informants might perceive as relevant in describing children's adjustment. From much factor-analytic work (some by Achenbach et al. using very large samples), it seems evident that there are both similarities and differences between subgroups in the underlying structure of child characteristics when samples are divided by age, gender, and informant. Selecting only factors common across such groups reduces the number of latent constructs to which one attends. Furthermore, although there are 216 items, chosen partly with an eye to breadth of content, these are probably still too few to represent every known syndrome well enough to yield a factor even within one particular segment of the population, much less a factor that is cross-age, cross-sex, and cross-informant. This is not a flaw of the ACQ, just a natural limitation. As an example, gender identity disorder is one syndrome whose absence jumped out because of some of my own previous work. Although there are several gender-deviance items in the ACQ, individually they did not differentiate the clinic and nonclinic groups, and collectively they apparently failed to form a sufficiently generalizable factor. Nevertheless, other research has established that gender problems can be assessed with the help of parent ratings (Bates & Bentler, 1973; Bates, Bentler, & Thompson, 1973; Meyer-Bahlberg, Feldman, & Ehrhardt, 1985; Zucker, Bradley, Doering, & Lozinski, 1985).[1]

Findings concerning the average differences in behavior problems and competencies seen in natural groups are also interesting, for more substantive reasons. Many of the differences that emerge would be expected, such as, for instance, the larger ratio of Externalizing to Internalizing symptoms shown by boys than by girls. However, the size of many of these differences might be a bit of a surprise to many readers. The clinic and normal samples are of course quite different on the main summary scores, and they differ across a very broad array of items. However, despite being highly reliable statistically, differences on items are for the most part relatively small. Similarly, although boys and girls are rated differently on many items, the size of difference is again small, and the differences in parents' ratings of children from different socioeconomic levels, ethnic groups, or regions of the country are even smaller. With the smaller differences, one is inclined to question the psychological meaningfulness of distinctions made between groups, as, for example, might be made concerning the incidence of behavior problems in different ethnic groups. For good scientific reasons, we usually focus on demonstrations of difference, but the present *Monograph*

---

[1] Why might a gender problem scale fail to appear in the ACQ? First, I see only three items that would be the core target for a gender problem factor, *2. Acts like opposite sex, 57. Dresses like or plays at being opposite sex,* and *209. Wishes to be of opposite sex.* When there are so few items, it would make it difficult (but not impossible) for a factor to emerge. In addition, these items might form a syndrome for boys, but they probably would not for girls, and they would be better at capturing a factor in younger than in older children.

reminds us that there could also be interesting nondifferences. While the minimal effects could be an artifact of the ACQ scale formats, I think that comparable research on the CBCL might lead to similar impressions about the smallness of group differences. I think that the minimal effect sizes have more to do with the broad and carefully stratified sampling than the questionnaire format.

Achenbach et al. also present interesting positive findings. For example, they show how family structure may be correlated with the child's adjustment: the larger the number of related adults living in the home, the better the child's adjustment. Conversely, the presence of more unrelated adults predicts poorer adjustment. The beneficial effect of related adults in the home goes beyond the single- versus the two-parent family. This is one of those findings that makes sense once demonstrated, but it is not one that had been widely reported previously (Achenbach et al. have not seen it previously, nor can I recall having seen this finding). Achenbach et al. attribute this effect to related adults playing a protective role beyond that of unrelated adults. They suggest that it may be due to deeper attachments to relatives. In addition, I might suggest that related adults are more likely to unite in efforts to control the child authoritatively because they have a greater emotional/social stake in the child's success. If these speculations are right, they might suggest actions for family therapists. Clinicians usually cannot do much about the socioeconomic stresses of a family, but with a skillful, focused effort they can sometimes amplify parent-child attachment bonds and effective parental control through structural interventions (Minuchin & Fishman, 1981). One might arrange, for example, for a peripheral father to take more salient, generationally appropriate roles with child and mother, even when he is away from the child's home. Less frequently, therapists call on grandparents and aunts and uncles to help, too. Even less often, they try to get unrelated members of the household relocated. The Achenbach et al. finding makes it more likely that I will consider such interventions, even though I recognize that the meaning of the finding needs to be established through further research.

There are two areas in which I would offer suggestions for future improvements in the line of work that is described in the *Monograph*. The first follows from some small doubts I have concerning the representativeness of the clinical sample used in this study. Using principles of survey research, Achenbach et al. systematically obtained a nationally representative sample of normal subjects; the corresponding sample of parental reports on clinical cases was also nationwide, and so large that the clinical cases were selected to match to the normal subjects demographically, rather than (as is common in most research) normal subjects being selected as matches to clinic subjects. However, the sites from which clinic subjects were gathered—to a large extent urban and university medical centers—may not be as systematically representative of the behavior problems of children of the whole nation. Achenbach et al. had good reasons for their sampling procedure, but one still wonders how representative this clinic sample is of the clientele of smaller-town clinics, of nonmedical child guidance centers, and of private practitioners. If fully representative national norms are the goal, then it would be good to attempt some resolution of this uncertainty in future research.

The second area, which ultimately is probably more important than the sampling of clinical cases, concerns the assessment of positive competencies. Achenbach et al. deserve praise for having long ago recognized that differences in the qualities of children's adjustment are not simply a function of the presence or absence of problem behaviors. Since recognition of this fact is only rarely reflected in research in the area of developmental psychopathology, Achenbach et al.'s strategy of pairing assessment of competencies with that of psychopathology is welcome. What is still absent in their work, however, is the same kind of systematic exploration of the positive competence domain as they undertook for the domain of negative behavior. The competence items of the ACQ do not reflect any differentiated theory of positive behavior, and it is impossible to judge whether a systematic sampling of relevant behaviors has been achieved. Factor analyses, such as those used originally to define syndromes of negative behaviors, have not been undertaken to determine subtypes of competent behavior. Neither is there any extensive attempt at validation of the competencies, except for treating them as alternate indexes of psychopathology, such as by comparing clinic and nonclinic sample mean scores. I believe that substantively interesting differences among positive competencies are to be found and that some of these competencies would emerge as relatively independent of the negative pathology dimensions. In my own work (e.g., Bates, Bayles, Bennett, Ridge, & Brown, 1991), some competency dimensions were indeed seen to be relatively independent of pathology. For example, the scale "Creative and Engaged" loaded moderately highly on a factor named "Active Engagement," which was defined by reports of a child's social activities and laboratory experimenter ratings of the child's sociability. "Creative and Engaged" loaded only very weakly on factors defined by teacher ratings of pathology (Academic-Social Competence) and maternal ratings of pathology (Maternal Perception of Personality/Adjustment).

I have covered here only a small sampling of the noteworthy findings and intriguing negative results reported in this *Monograph*. An earlier *Monograph* by Achenbach and Edelbrock (1981) served as a valuable source for child psychopathology researchers of the 1980s. Although it is too soon to tell whether this *Monograph* will be equally valuable, I think it is safe to predict that it will stay on the desks of many scholars for a long time.

References

Achenbach, T. M., Conners, C. K., Quay, H. C., Verhulst, F. C., & Howell, C. T. (1989). Replication of empirically derived syndromes as a basis for taxonomy of child/adolescent psychopathology. *Journal of Abnormal Child Psychology, 17,* 299–323.

Achenbach, T. M., & Edelbrock, C. (1981). Behavioral problems and competencies reported by parents of normal and disturbed children aged four to sixteen. *Monographs of the Society for Research in Child Development,* **46**(1, Serial No. 188).

Bates, J. E., Bayles, K., Bennett, D. S., Ridge, B., & Brown, M. M. (1991). Origins of externalizing behavior problems at eight years of age. In D. J. Pepler & K. H. Rubin (Eds.), *The development and treatment of childhood aggression* (pp. 93–120). Hillsdale, NJ: Erlbaum.

Bates, J. E., & Bentler, P. M. (1973). Play activities of normal and effeminate boys. *Developmental Psychology,* **9,** 20–27.

Bates, J. E., Bentler, P. M., & Thompson, S. K. (1973). Measurement of deviant gender development in boys. *Child Development,* **44,** 591–598.

Meyer-Bahlburg, H. F. L., Feldman, J. F., & Ehrhardt, A. A. (1985). Questionnaires for the assessment of atypical gender role behavior: A methodological study. *Journal of the American Academy of Child Psychiatry,* **24,** 695–701.

Minuchin, S., & Fishman, H. C. (1981). *Family therapy techniques.* Cambridge, MA: Harvard University Press.

Zucker, K. J., Bradley, S. J., Doering, R. W., & Lozinski, J. A. (1985). Sex-typed behavior in cross-gender-identified children: Stability and change at one-year follow-up. *Journal of the American Academy of Child Psychiatry,* **24,** 710–719.

We are grateful to John E. Bates for his eloquent Commentary as well as for his constructive reviews of the drafts of this *Monograph*. As both commentator and editorial reviewer, he has illuminated and amplified our work. His perspective is helpful in reflecting back to us the impressions that this work makes on others. We especially appreciate his recognition of the relations between the "many psychometric facts" and the "broader methodological approach and theoretical perspective."

In efforts to advance the developmental study of psychopathology, there has been a tendency to focus either on psychometric facts or on theoretical perspectives with insufficient attention to the relations between them. We feel that psychometric facts and theoretical perspectives are both essential for the developmental study of psychopathology.

The ACQ grew out of our work as an American Psychological Association task force charged with exploring the prospects for an empirically based taxonomy of children's behavior problems. There had already been numerous efforts to identify syndromes by means of multivariate analyses. However, we decided that it was time to move this approach into a "second-generation" phase by subjecting syndromes hypothesized from the first-generation efforts to a more comprehensive test than had been done before.

We chose parent ratings as our starting point, but this did not mean that we believed that parents should be the sole source of data either for the assessment of individual children or for the identification of syndromes. Instead, we invested in a particular methodological and theoretical approach as one of many possible ways to advance both the psychometrics and the concepts of child psychopathology. The syndromes we found in the ACQ clinical samples and their agreement with syndromes from other clinical samples supported some but not all of the syndromes that we had hypothesized from the first-generation studies (Achenbach, Conners, Quay, Verhulst, & Howell, 1989). Some of the ACQ syndromes were quite similar for both sexes and different ages, but other syndromes were found for only one sex or for a limited age range.

Bates raises the question of why a gender problems scale might fail to appear in the ACQ. In fact, one of the syndromes that we found for only one sex in one age range did include problems of gender identity, plus other problems related to sexuality (Achenbach et al., 1989). Because our current *Monograph* focused only on those syndromes that were found for both sexes and multiple age ranges, we did not include the Sex Problems syndrome here. However, Bates's question about a gender problems syndrome raises the more general issue of whether additional syndromes could have been found if additional items were included in the ACQ.

Our selection of items was designed to tap 12 syndromes (including a Sex Problems syndrome) hypothesized from previous multivariate research. We also included numerous additional items that were considered intrinsically important, even though we did not hypothesize that they would be associated primarily with one syndrome. Nevertheless, our failure to find a particular syndrome in parents' ACQ ratings does not necessarily mean that the syndrome could not be found by other means. Furthermore, the syndromes derived from parents' ratings should not necessarily be the sole basis for taxonomic constructs. Subsequent research has now added syndromes derived empirically from teacher and self-ratings as a basis for defining the eight syndrome constructs analyzed in the current *Monograph* (Achenbach, 1991). This research has also identified a Self-Destructive/Identity Problems syndrome in self-ratings by adolescent boys that was not identified in parent or teacher ratings in addition to supporting the Sex Problems syndrome in parents' ratings of younger children.

Although findings were not available in time for the current *Monograph*, we have conducted a longitudinal reassessment of our national sample 3 years after the initial assessment and will soon conduct a 6-year reassessment. Both reassessments include reports by teachers and the subjects themselves as well as by parents. The sampling, the psychometrics, and the findings reported here thus provide a foundation for studying the subsequent development of psychopathology as assessed from multiple sources (McConaughy, Stanger, & Achenbach, in press; Stanger, McConaughy, & Achenbach, in press).

References

Achenbach, T. M. (1991). *Integrative guide for the 1991 CBCL/4–18, YSR, and TRF profiles.* Burlington: University of Vermont, Department of Psychiatry.
Achenbach, T. M., Conners, C. K., Quay, H. C., Verhulst, F. C., & Howell, C. T. (1989).

Replication of empirically derived syndromes as a basis for taxonomy of child/adolescent psychopathology. *Journal of Abnormal Child Psychology,* **17,** 299–323.

McConaughy, S. H., Stanger, C., & Achenbach, T. M. (in press). Three-year course of behavioral/emotional problems in a national sample of 4- to 16-year olds: 1. Agreement among informants. *Journal of the American Academy of Child and Adolescent Psychiatry.*

Stanger, C., McConaughy, S. H., & Achenbach, T. M. (in press). Three-year course of behavioral/emotional problems in a national sample of 4- to 16-year-olds: 2. Predictors of syndromes. *Journal of the American Academy of Child and Adolescent Psychiatry.*

CONTRIBUTORS

Thomas M. Achenbach (Ph.D. 1966, University of Minnesota) is professor and director of the Center for Children, Youth, and Families at the University of Vermont Department of Psychiatry. His research interests include assessment, taxonomy, and epidemiology of psychopathology, relations between development and psychopathology, and long-term outcomes of childhood problems.

Catherine T. Howell (M.S. 1967, Tulane University) is psychometrician and data manager in the Center for Children, Youth, and Families of the University of Vermont Department of Psychiatry. Her work focuses on the management and analysis of longitudinal data on children's interests, competencies, and behavioral/emotional problems.

Herbert C. Quay (Ph.D. 1958, University of Illinois) is professor and chair of the Department of Psychology at the University of Miami. He is also editor of the *Journal of Abnormal Child Psychology*. His research interests include juvenile delinquency and the origins of socialized and undersocialized aggressive conduct disorders.

C. Keith Conners (Ph.D. 1960, Harvard University) is professor of psychiatry at Duke University. His current research focuses on cognitive processes in reading disorders, the effects of cognition-enhancing medication on young adult dyslexics, and the assessment of attention-deficit and learning disorders.

John E. Bates (Ph.D. 1973, University of California, Los Angeles) is professor of psychology at Indiana University. His research is primarily on how individual differences arise in children's styles of behavioral or emotional adjustment, with special focus on the roles of child temperament, parent-child relations, and family stress. His clinical practice is mainly with families solving child and adolescent behavior problems.

STATEMENT OF EDITORIAL POLICY

The *Monographs* series is intended as an outlet for major reports of developmental research that generate authoritative new findings and use these to foster a fresh and/or better-integrated perspective on some conceptually significant issue or controversy. Submissions from programmatic research projects are particularly welcome; these may consist of individually or group-authored reports of findings from some single large-scale investigation or of a sequence of experiments centering on some particular question. Multiauthored sets of independent studies that center on the same underlying question can also be appropriate; a critical requirement in such instances is that the various authors address common issues and that the contribution arising from the set as a whole be both unique and substantial. In essence, irrespective of how it may be framed, any work that contributes significant data and/or extends developmental thinking will be taken under editorial consideration.

Submissions should contain a minimum of 80 manuscript pages (including tables and references); the upper limit of 150–175 pages is much more flexible (please submit four copies; a copy of every submission and associated correspondence is deposited eventually in the archives of the SRCD). Neither membership in the Society for Research in Child Development nor affiliation with the academic discipline of psychology are relevant; the significance of the work in extending developmental theory and in contributing new empirical information is by far the most crucial consideration. Because the aim of the series is not only to advance knowledge on specialized topics but also to enhance cross-fertilization among disciplines or subfields, it is important that the links between the specific issues under study and larger questions relating to developmental processes emerge as clearly to the general reader as to specialists on the given topic.

Potential authors who may be unsure whether the manuscript they are planning would make an appropriate submission are invited to draft an outline of what they propose and send it to the Editor for assessment.

This mechanism, as well as a more detailed description of all editorial policies, evaluation processes, and format requirements, is given in the "Guidelines for the Preparation of *Monographs* Submissions," which can be obtained by writing to Wanda C. Bronson, Institute of Human Development, 1203 Tolman Hall, University of California, Berkeley, CA 94720.